It's Not What You Think

A Collection of Flash Fiction Stories

by Gary Zenker

White Lightning Publishing

The work in this book is fiction and you can't prove otherwise, even if you think that the main character in the story is based on you. Any references to real places are used fictionally, even the bathroom mentions. Names, characters, fictitious places and events are the products of the author's imagination. Any resemblance to actual persons, living or dead, your crazy Aunt Jane, your son, your dog, your neighbor's dog or even you is purely a coincidence or likely the result of an LSD flashback and honestly, if that is the case how could you know whether any of that is true? No matter what you think, I'll claim it isn't. Nah nah nah nah nah.

For more information, requests for presentations, permissions for reprints, interviews, opportunities for Gary to lounge in your living room and eat all your leftovers with his dirty shoes on your sofa, or other equally unpleasant outcomes, please contact him at *garyzenker@gmail.com*.

White Lightning Publishing

ISBN 978-1-941028-34-6

CONTENTS

INTRODUCTION

The danger of writing flash fiction – most often defined as stories of one thousand words and under – is that your collection introduction can end up being longer than some or all of your stories. There's irony for you.

I tell anyone who will listen that flash fiction is like swiss cheese. How well it stands depends on the placement of the holes within it. With the word limitations, the skilled writer decides which details to put in and which to let the readers fill in for themselves.

I admire my friends and peers who plan and write stories of 135,000 or more words incorporating lush descriptions and draw a world which we can see, feel, smell, hear and touch. But the skill of telling a flash fiction story, with just a fraction of that total word count, requires skills that are nearly a polar opposite: knowing what details to *leave out* and still create a believable world.

Well-constructed flash fiction requires what any and every well-told story requires: character, plot, pacing, conflict and resolution of some sort. Given the restricted number of words involved, it necessitates exceptional story-telling skill. By the time the novelist is just setting the scene, the flash fiction writer has already made you like the characters, introduced a problem and brought it to resolution.

Some people ask whether my stories are real. Some of my stories are based on real events or characters. *Soup for One* is 99% how the actual conversation occurred with my son (feel free to feel sorry for him). Others, like *Crazy Love*, are based on the merest of fleeting thoughts or feelings, using "what if" as my writing guide (thank goodness). Most often, the stories contain a variety of observations from real experiences expanded, exaggerated or otherwise moved from one situation and applied to a fictional one.

This volume contains short stories covering a variety of topics and genre. Some are dialog based and others are primarily the thoughts of the protagonist. Think of it like a box of mixed chocolates: you'll like some more than the others. That's okay…I feel the same way.

I hope that the stories presented will draw you into the situation and the characters involved. I like to incorporate an underlying theme of human nature or behavior into my stories and, sometimes, play with the readers' emotions. Getting someone to laugh or cry with just my words is an amazing feeling of accomplishment.

Some of my readers have asked "what happens next?" to the characters or suggest how great it would be to expand it or keep it going. It's a great compliment that they want more, but I hardly ever do it. I enjoy the challenge of using fewer rather than more words in storytelling. And once I have told the story that I wanted to tell, my part in the process is over. What happens next is for *you* to imagine.

If you find yourself surprised at the twist in a story you didn't expect, it makes me happy. Again, it complements my skills as a storyteller. And in case you wonder, I purposely leave a few vague elements about a character or detail so that you and another reader might draw different conclusions. That's part of the swiss cheese nature of my writing and having fun with the reader.

And before you word-counters call me on it, I guess I should also admit that some of the stories included extend beyond the thousand-word limit generally used to define flash fiction. They are still short as compared to the normal definition of short stories. I believe you should use the words you need to tell your story, and a few of these needed a bit more than a thousand.

I'd love your feedback and to read your thoughts on which stories are your favorites *and why*. Feel free to email me at garyzenker@gmail.com.

Gary Zenker
October 2017

CRITIQUE

I want to write like Tina does, in sentences that flow together in rhythmic perfection. I want to use prose that makes my reader taste the traces of oak in the red wine and smell the slightly sweet scent of burning candle wax. I want them to feel the incredible softness of the satin sheets she describes as her characters make love between them. I want people to read my words and place themselves in the middle of an argument between two people and have the anger envelope and overtake them.

But that doesn't happen; it never happens when people read **my** work. The members of my critique group stare politely at the double-spaced pages I have handed them, listening as I read my words that have been carefully assembled into complex and thought-provoking sentences. They shift a bit in their seats as I read, but there are no giggles at the humorous parts; no nods at the detailed descriptions and no gasps at the plot reveals.

These people are friendly and chatty **before** they read my piece. They smile and ask about my children, my dog, and my job. But once we begin the critique, they change. They tear apart my characters, stab holes in my plot line, nitpick at my word choice, and otherwise unravel my carefully constructed work into a pile of junkyard rejects displayed with no rhyme, reason or purpose. I am ashamed, embarrassed and lost. And still I come back each month hoping to catch the smallest of compliments or a token of recognition for the talent that lies within me.

So I read my newest work out loud with a mix of defiance and trepidation. I have placed my best work and skill into the words I've selected. I've gone over it several dozen times, changing the scene, changing the characters, changing the plot. I've subtracted words, replaced others and changed them back again. And I know exactly what to expect the moment that the first person opens her mouth.

"So, on page one," Tina, the lady to my left begins her critique 'sandwich'. I stop her mid-sentence with the short but sharp knife I pull from my pocket, quickly swinging my arm to rest it against her throat. I see the fear in her eyes three seconds before they roll back into her head as my knife slices through her skin like carving a turkey. Blood spurts out in an arc, soaking the face and glasses of the old man across from her.

Faster than he can react, I slam the point of the same knife through his right hand, trapping it on my five pages covered with the blue ink markings he made while I read my work aloud. I shift behind the man to his left. He writes the poetry everyone raves about that I still cannot understand.

"And ***your*** critique?" I growl into his right ear from

behind, my chin pressing against the side of his face and his grey beard.

"I...I...I..." he stammers at a loss for words. Just as I suspected. He hates it. I tilt my head slightly and bear my teeth down on his scrawny, wrinkled neck. I clamp down and rip away as much flesh as I can manage, spitting it onto the table. Can anyone else understand what he's trying to say? I know I can't. But there's no one left to answer me.

That's because "Hi! My Name Is Charlie," sitting across from me, appears to have had a heart attack between the time I sliced Tina and incapacitated Edward knife-in-the-hand. All without a single kind word. How rude. Serves him right, I say.

Blood runs off the table and pools on the floor. It's a mess but that's why you have a waitress, right? I could really use a glass of water about now. She really isn't doing much to earn her tip.

I look to the other tables and their critiques. They are continuing without interruption. People are reading out loud while others offer commentary. There's laughter. They're engrossed in the pieces there and ignoring what goes on at my table. No one is even looking our way. I sit back down in my seat and draw a deep breath. "Maybe," I speak out loud to the people at my table who can no longer hear me, "Maybe if I read this again... you will appreciate it better." I focus only on the paper, channeling my author inner-self. I start reading my piece again from the very beginning, changing the emphasis on some of the words. Yes, this reading was much better. I close my eyes and take the quiet moment to reflect.

"Gary, are you okay? I didn't hurt your feelings, did I?" Tina-to-my-left asks. Her voice is soft and offers true concern.

I take a second deep breath before finally opening my eyes. "Yeah, I'm fine," I answer slowly, turning my head to look her in the eyes. "I just have a hard time with criticism."

Watch the author read this story:
https://www.youtube.com
/watch?v=UBWIKF3kQ4M

Author's notes: *Having led and participated in hundreds of critique sessions, I wanted to offer a little fantasy for all the writers who survive them. It takes incredibly brave people to bring something they have labored on, purposefully asking for other people to rip it apart.*

People don't view me the same way after they read this piece. It was one of several attempts to start a story one way, switch genre midstream and surprise the reader.

Originally published in Running Wild Anthology of Short Stories Volume 1.

SOUP FOR ONE

"Do you have something you want to tell me?" I ask my ten year old son Seth. He's at an age where he past wanting to tell me about his school day but not past the age where a teacher will send me a note to tell me about a behavioral issue at school.

"About what?"

"I don't know. Maybe about music class since it seems I have an email from your teacher that I haven't opened yet."

"Oh that" he says dismissively. "She is old and cranky."

"Then you DO have something to tell me?"

"They are making us dance in music class," he informs with clear disgust in his voice. "So there's a song that we dance to that says we get no soup. It's part of the words. So I pretended to be eating soup."

I look at my sister without breaking a smile but she can see the glint in my eyes and knows what comes next.

"I see," I nodded. "So before I read her email, was there anything else?" I asked.

"No. We were just twirling around. It's a dance for the spring fair. I pretended to eat soup so she made me sit down. I don't care."

This is the same teacher that, the last time she sent me a note, had made Seth sit down away from the other kids because he pretended to play a tuba. A tuba. Not a flute. Not the drums. Not a guitar. He was playing air tuba. I would have thought she would have rewarded him for his imagination or at least kept him for the air instrument band. After all, how many air tuba players can there be at that school?

"So let me ask you some questions. What kind of soup was it?"

"I don't know."

"You don't know what kind of soup you were pretending to eat? Really? Well, was it a cup or a bowl?"

"I don't know."

"Hmm. You don't know?"

"I don't know."

"Well, was it hot or cold soup? Some soups you eat cold."

“I don't know, it was pretend soup.”

“Hmmmm. Show me what you did.”

He shows me and pretends to eat some soup in the air.

“So you were using a spoon!”

“Yeah, I guess so.”

“But you don't know what kind of soup it was and whether it was a cup or a bowl?”

“It doesn't matter,” he raises his voice. “I got in trouble.”

“Well, are you sure you didn't do anything else?” I pulled up her email on the phone and read it. “She says that you were twirling around and bumping into people.”

“We are supposed to twist when we dance. I wasn't *banging* into people.”

“Hmmmm. Did you spill soup on anyone?”

“It wasn’t real soup.”

“I just thought maybe someone got stains on their clothing or got burned on the soup. Maybe someone slipped in it on the floor?”

"It was pretend soup! I hate you. I got in trouble and you are making fun of me."

"I am not making fun of you. I am just asking questions so I know the situation."

"Don't talk to me any more."

"Ok, it's time for bed anyway. Go get changed." I stood and looked at my sister while he clomped away.

"You know," she said, "you won't be able to make him take it seriously if you do that."

"How seriously can you take it if you get in trouble from a music teacher for pretending to eat soup? He is ten. She is lucky that's all he does in class."

"You may just want to remind him that she is the teacher and he needs to take her direction."

"Okay, Mom."

"I'm just saying."

"Okay." I walk upstairs. It's hard to make a federal case out of this. Was this really worth an email? My son forgets to hand in four homeworks in a week and I don't get an email, but I get one for this? He's in the bed and I sit on the edge of it.

“You know you need to apologize to your teacher tomorrow. She's trying to manage 20 kids and you are causing a disruption.”

“Do I have to?”

“Yes.”

“Okay, I will.”

“Good boy.” I move to him and kiss him on the forehead. “And you know that you cannot tell her you are sorry because you know there is no eating in class?”

“Yes I know,” he replies in that way ten year kids have.

“Ok, goodnight” I tell him and walk away. But I stop just outside the doorway. “Crackers?”

“What?” Seth asks me

“Crackers. Was it just soup or did you have crackers, too?”

He rolls over to face the other way without us saying another word.

Watch the author read the story:

https://www.youtube.com/watch?v=CAXilv-sOGA&t=84s

Author's notes: *It's important for the reader to realize that, except for the very last lines, this is exactly how the conversation went between me and my son. I basically retraced the conversation after putting him to bed and got it down in a tangible format.*

It's a lesson that writers are always writing, even in their live conversations with others. Also, it proves that having a parent who is a writer may be the worst situation in which any child can find him or herself.

HELLO MY NAME IS...

My eyes focused on his lapel and name tag. It read "Hello, my name is…Asshole."

Actually, his name tag read "Hello my name is…Ronnie Shearer, but it could have read Asshole and been just as accurate. I'd known Ronnie back in high school where most of the kids ARE assholes of one sort or another. It wasn't as great an accomplishment as it is when they are older. Teenagers lead self-centered, drama-laden lives that only intersect with others so that they can get stoned, get laid, hassle others or pick up the opposite sex to facilitate the first two. In that world, Ronnie was an outstanding achiever.

In those high school days, I was one of his frequent victims. He wouldn't recognize me today. I lost 50 pounds, my acne cleared up, I replaced my glasses with contacts and my shoulder-length-covering-my-face hair is now a short, middle-aged cut.

Already face-to-face with him at this business mixer, I do the only adult thing possible: I stick out my hand to shake Asshole's hand. "Hi, Ronnie," I say while raising an eyebrow just slightly in anticipation of being recognized. I'm not. His eyes go immediately to my nametag which is conveniently left blank.

"You know, you're supposed to write your name in the white area," he smirks.

"Oh, well." I lower my gaze, transported momentarily back to high school. I raise my face and look him straight in the eyes. "I'm in the middle of changing my name and I wasn't sure whether to use my old or new name."

"Witness protection program?" You don't look the type."

I spontaneously decide to create some backstory. "I think I should use my new name. Francois Dubois. It's *of the woods*," I said, using my complete knowledge of the French language.

"Did you pick that name or was it forced on you?" he pushes.

"It's my Farbera name. Given to me by my sponsors. You know Farbera, right?"

"I've heard of it," he lies. Same old Ronnie. He gives me permission to take this as far as I can.

"Of course. Farbera is the belief that all physical things not ony have a spiritual element but also hold power over the six senses." It sounds pretty reasonable to me as I say it, so I nod to myself.

"There are only five senses."

"In Farbera, there is a sixth, Mentalisha." I repeat the last work again in an attempt to actually remember it for later in the conversation. "It refers to the ability to see or feel an aura of sexuality around others. These girls make the girls from the seventies look like nuns. As long as you are a believer…" I pause for effect. He doesn't say a word. "Really. Everyone makes love to everyone, as often as possible. One night stands are encouraged. Drinking is fine," I note while looking at the wine glass in his hand. "But they don't believe in drugs at all. Just wine and sex and lots of it. Sex makes you holy."

"Farbera girls," he repeats and chugs his wine. I know it's time to close the sale.

"There's just one thing. Farbera guys and girls are forbidden to talk openly about their belief." I realize the incongruence of telling him this and stop there, hoping he doesn't catch on. He was never that smart, anyway.

"Kind of like wearing a face covering?" he asks. He's making this too easy for me.

"Yeah, just like that. So you can't ask directly if they are believers."

"So how do you know who's who? Do you all go to the same church?"

"You can but men and women sit on opposite sides of the hall and you can't talk to them. And there's no sex on that day. The way you discover it is this..." I lean into him and lower my voice. "You kiss her and grab her ass. When they kiss back, you know they are Farbera. Who else would do that on first meeting except Farbera women?" I pull back and look at him. He's on the edge – he wants to buy in but needs one last convincing push.

Conveniently, my girlfriend walks up to me with a glass of wine. I encircle her waist with my arm and pull her into me. I push my mouth onto hers and grab her ass. I break quickly and whisper in her ear "play this with me."

"Hi, I'm Francois," I say without the crack of a smile. "Would you like to get together later to check my aura?"

"Sure. I'm Janet. I would like that," she replies. "I need to talk to a few more people but right after would be great." She walks off, putting extra sway into her movements. God, I love that woman.

Ronnie's mouth is half open as he takes it all in and becomes a Farbera believer on the spot. "I recognize three of the girls in that group over there," I point in the general direction of people I've never met. "The blonde is amazing." Without another word, he walks off to join them.

Suddenly I have a terrible thought. Maybe I am the Asshole. Who else would hold a grudge from high school and fabricate a ridiculous story like I did? What kind of person am I to want to embarrass someone in the present for past behaviors that they have probably outgrown?

As I have these terrible thoughts, a guy walks up to me and sticks out his hand. "Hey, I was talking to Ronnie earlier. He pointed at you and bet me ten bucks that if he pretended to be gay, you would hit on him. But I saw you with that hot chick, so I guess I win the ten." He slapped me on the shoulder.

Suddenly, I'm not feeling so bad. I turn just in time to see Ronnie with a handful of the blonde's ass and her hauling off and slapping him hard. The room goes silent with eye on them. Nope, not feeling badly about it at all.

I walk over to Janet and take her hand. "Time to go, love," and we head for the door.

Author's notes: *Fictional, but we've all been to enough reunions to know that it isn't completely out of the question that we would like to see this happen.*

ARE WE THERE YET?

"Are we there yet?" my son Seth asks for what seems to be the fiftieth time in under ten minutes. These three words, universally applied by children of every age and culture, are like the constant pressure of water against hardened stone that eventually helped to created the Grand Canyon.

My knuckles whiten from my tightened grip on the steering wheel. If I didn't need them locked on the wheel, I would reach back and strangle the breath from the son I love more than life. I'm sure he knows it.

"No, for the fortieth time," I reply and try to place myself, mentally at least, in my happy place. Not the Grand Canyon…which might have been it *before* having a child.

"I don't think it's the fortieth. More like only the twelfth," he accounts back. The kid who can't remember that Tuesday and Friday every week are trash days, who can't remember to brush his teeth on waking up and going to sleep, and can't remember to put on fresh underwear each day, has a rainman-like ability to remember the exact number of times I have already said no. I tell myself that I need to take him to Vegas and card count while I play blackjack.

“Twelfth or fortieth, the answer is still no.” He sits back in what would appear to the casual observer as retreat. Any parent knows it is really tactical reformation.

Before you have children of your own, you see their logic as amusing, even admirable. Once you have them, you see them as God’s revenge for every infraction you’ve made against your family, friends, strangers and maybe a small dog named Prince who you punished after chewing one of your celebrity branded sneakers as a youth.

“Are we there yet?” he breaks the 45 seconds of sweet silence. I feign deafness and turn up the volume on the radio. He repeats the phrase louder, twice. I’m still in silent mode, humming to the music.

“Dad. Can you turn down the radio for a second?” I do as requested. “Dad!” he repeats.

“What?”

“Suppose I was choking and needed help. If you don’t answer me and ask me what, I could die.”

“You weren’t choking.”

“But I could have been. See, I was chewing on this straw.” I adjust the rear view mirror to place him directly in view and he holds the gnarled piece of white plastic up for me to see.

“Stop chewing on the straw, then.”

“I coulda died.” I am wondering if I will live long enough to get to where we are going. “But you don’t care if I die…" And there it is, the guilt play. He's on a roll. "I wonder who I should leave all my baseball cards to?" It's the very same play I used to use against my own parents, 40 years ago. Social media may have changed **where** we say things, but not what we say.

"Leave them to me. I'll throw them away. Your room is a mess anyway and I could clean it out and use it for a work room." The silence that follows is golden but I decide to use the opportunity to have a meaningful conversation with him.

"Do you want to be buried or cremated?" I ask, looking him in the eye through the rearview mirror. "Or I could donate your body to science. They could use your body parts for experiments. I wonder what they would do with your brain."

"You're the meanest father ever," he observes. If I weren't driving to Disney, I might agree. Might. I am hoping that the car vibrations and the conversation takes its toll on him. It does. Through the rearview mirror, I can see his head start to sway a bit. His eyes start to flutter and a moment later, he is out. Thank goodness.

I try to focus my attention on the road ahead but miss a huge pothole, hitting it directly. It rocks the car and I pray like I have never prayed before that my son stays asleep. He does.

I start humming again to the radio when, without warning, the *other* groggy little voice from the back seat, his cousin, speaks up. "Are we there yet?"

Author's notes: *We all know what the teenage years bring, how we ourselves behaved and how our own children are likely to be. So it isn't unreasonable for parents to flex our influence and inflict some hassle into their lives ahead of time. Then we have something we can look back on and smile at when they later do the same to us.*

SELF RESTRAINT

There are two kinds of sex. One is the kind where you do it to merge with your partner completely, in mind and soul. You become perfectly connected and in synch. You stare into your partner's eyes and want the moment to never end. You think about intertwining wrinkled fingers and walking slowly down the park sidewalk fifty years into the future.

This wasn't that type of sex.

"Wow, I'm hungry" she said, lifting her back from the bed for the first time in the last ten minutes. "And thirsty. I need water. Want any?"

"Sure. But would you mind undoing the wrist cuff first? I have to check my phone messages."

"Oh yeah." The ripping sound of velcro filled my left ear and I rubbed my wrist from where the too-tight cuff had been.

"When did you get this strapped on…and how?" I asked her.

"Somewhere between 'oh' and 'oooohhhhhhh' I think. You were otherwise pre-occupied."

I didn't remember that, nor could I remember when the wine spilled down the comforter and puddled onto the rug. The phone binged with a new text message. I reached on the floor for the iPhone, scooped it up and pushed a couple of buttons. I tried to block out the sound of her releasing a stream like a racehorse as I read the text messages.

“Hey, it’s Tim. I’m back in town two days earlier than expected. Meet you at your place at 9. Kiss kiss.” I pulled the phone from my ear and checked the timing of the phone call. 8:45. Her phone, not mine. I pursed my lips even though no one would be able to see.

“Hey Connie. That Tim you have been talking about is coming over at 9.”

“What time is it now?”

“8:45…maybe 8:46 now.”

“Shit. He doesn’t know that you and I …”

“He doesn’t know that you and I …” I repeated exactly as she had said it.

“Are you making fun of me?” she walked into the room, thong in redress position and sat on the bed. She was stunning and probably out of my class. Although my one talent does help me jump to a higher class… “Are you making fun of me?” she asked again.

“Probably. It’s what I do. So we have like 15 minutes to make sure he can’t tell we had sex. Think that’s possible?

“I don’t know, how does my hair look?”

"You're doomed. How about me?"

"If you had any, you might be in trouble."

"Nice. I spend 10 minutes nearly suffocating for YOUR pleasure and you make jokes about my slightly thinning hair?"

"Pretty much. Go use the brush in the bathroom," she suggested.

"Chances are I won't be able to leave here before he gets here. I never met your Tim."

"Well today, I guess you get to meet him."

I walked out back to the room. "How's my breath?" and I blew some air in her face.

"Brush your teeth. Please. Use any brush you find there, even the hair brush."

I looked at her funny. "I'm interested in getting things out…"

"I know what you are going to say, funny boy. Just brush. You know, you're lucky I'm an easy lay."

"So what have you told your Tim about me?"

"Nothing. Why would YOU come up?" I snickered at the play on words but at the same time winced at the implication. I wasn't important enough to be part of a real conversation with a real person in her life. "He's a very straight guy. He wouldn't want to know his girlfriend plays on the side every once in a while."

"Once in a while? This is the third time this week. You're lucky I can keep…up."

"Sounds like you're the lucky one." She smiled and kissed me lightly on the lips. Suddenly, for a moment, for the first time, I was jealous, which was against the rules of casual sex. No jealousy, no commitment, no nothing. Just fun fun fun and go go go. And now something was happening that I couldn't control. It lasted more than just a moment.

"Are you okay?" She gave me a funny look. "Are you nervous about meeting Tim. Or are you…having second thoughts about this casual thing?" she questioned with a smile that I don't think I had ever seen on her before. It was a quirky smile that made me feel…different.

"No…yes…maybe. We've always been honest with each other. I'm not sure how I feel… Yes, yes, I don't like this casual thing."

"What would you like to do about it?" she asked me. The pause lasted half a minute.

"I want to date you exclusively," I blurted before I could retract the words. We stared at each other, both with surprised looks on our faces.

"What about all of your other girlfriends?"

"I haven't been with anyone else in over three months. Anyway, given the number of nights you've had me on call, I wouldn't have had the time. Or the strength."

"Are you saying that I've been needy?"

"No…yes…I don't know. I just know that I've really liked spending time with you and I really hate the fact that Tim is coming over and that I have to leave."

"When did this happen?"

"I don't know. Sometime between 'oh' and 'ooohhhh' I guess." She laughed at me.

"Well, we do get along fairly well and Tim only drops in town once a month. You would definitely be more reliable."

"What will you do about Tim?"

"I'll text him and tell him I'm staying at a girlfriend's and meet him tomorrow for brunch and break it off with him then. Is that okay?"

"You really want to do that?"

"Well, is that what YOU want?"

Deep breath. Complete change of life. "Yes. Yes it is."

"Then get your pants off and get back into bed. Mister. If we are going to have a real relationship, I'm going to make you work for it." She texted a message and dropped the phone on the nightstand to march back into the bathroom. "Out in a minute," she called to me.

The phone gave a bing, indicating a text message received. Probably from Tim in response to her text. Since I was now her boyfriend, I felt it reasonable to see what her newly ex-boyfriended Tim wrote. "Told you it would work out like that. He just needed a little push. See you at brunch tomorrow. Helena."

I re-read it twice before I understood it fully. Then I shuffled under the sheets and found the wrist restraints. I wasn't going to be the only one tied down in this relationship.

Watch the author read the story:

https://www.youtube.com/watch?v=nPq5QlSPnWc&t=266s

Author's notes: *While guys think we are masters of the game, women know that they truly control it all.*

STOLEN MEMORIES

That smell! It's obvious that Little Johnny's diaper is full and needs changing. I don't see him but he's in the room somewhere, that much I know. I start to yell for him and my wife but my voice comes out more as a harsh bark.

How long have I had this cold affecting my voice? A week? Two weeks? I can't really remember. Maybe it was when I gave Little Johnny my keys to play with. Kids that age are walking …crap, what is the word for it? You know, that thing in a lab where they grow all the germs on purpose. It'll come back to me.

Anyway, the kids are germ carriers. At one point I was sick for a year, right after he started daycare. I thought I had the big A or cancer or something. I'd never been so sick in my life…that I could remember, anyway.

I smell that dirty diaper again. "Johnny," comes out a little easier this time. The chair is comfy and I don't really feel like getting up. There's a guy sitting across from me. He looks familiar.

"Are you okay?" he asks me. I nod. My throat is still sore. I see my cup with a blue bendy straw on the table beside me. I reach over toward it but must have misjudged the distance without my glasses and knock the whole thing onto the floor. The liquid spreads out and runs across the linoleum. Petri dish. That's the phrase…a petri dish.

"That's okay, I'll get that. How was your nap?"

"Fine," I croak out as he grabs half a box of tissues. "Have you seen Myra?"

"She's here somewhere," the guy says as he finishes wiping up the spill. Yesterday she came back from the store with Moon Pies. I love Moon Pies. And a cake for Little Johnny's birthday. She needed nearly a whole box of candles since we couldn't find any of the old ones. "Thirteen going on thirty" she joked, and she is right. I don't tell her that before she returned with the cake, he was smoking out in the garage. Or that he had gotten into my beer stash.

"Tell her she needs to change Little Johnny's diaper, it stinks." She hates changing diapers, says that the smell makes her gag. Who ever heard of a mother who didn't change diapers? Pain in the ass, that's what it is. So sometimes I just wait her out so she's forced to do it.

The young man stands up and throws the used tissues in the trash can. He pours water from the pitcher into my cup.

"Thank you." He walks over to my bureau and picks up an object sitting there. It's a paper weight that my boy got me on his field trip to the Smithsonian. A fish in a Lucite block. It's completely clouded and broke in half. But he was so excited the day he brought it home for me, so I've kept it. "Don't worry. It was broke before. You didn't do it. Someone gave it to me. But it's old like me." Old like me? When did I get old. I still don't remember that exact moment.

"I'm going to have to go back to the job soon. It's been a nice vacation week but….have you seen Myra?"

"She's around somewhere" but he doesn't look for her.

"Tell her I'm ready to go to the restaurant. They don't have room service at this hotel, do they?"

"I don't think so."

"Johnny," I say and look at him. He smiles back at me. "It's okay. It's nice of you to come all this way to see your old man. You know, Mom talks to me in my dreams. She's watching over us. She told me so."

Johnny starts to tear up a little. I want to stand up and hug him but these old legs of mine are practically useless. "I'm in The Home, aren't I?" He nods.

The room is confusing. It's not my living room. It's familiar. It's got some of my stuff, photos of my family. Myra, Little Johnny and me together. I forget who took that one. The guy in front of the bureau is holding the thing Little Johnny gave me.

I scream. “Hey you. Put that down. That’s mine. My son gave that to me.” He stares at me a second and then puts it back down on the counter. “Look, you broke it. My son gave that to me and you broke it. Go on, get out of here.” He looks at me a minute and starts talking gibberish. I’m mad. A lady dressed in white comes in the room and whispers to him. They’re talking about me, I know it. “Get out of here, both of you. Why do people keep walking into my place. I oughta call the police. Leave,” I scream as loud as I can and start coughing so hard my back hurts. They look at me and finally leave.

I try to push myself up in the chair but I’m so tired that I can’t manage it. I see the broken gift on my counter and start to cry. Damn strangers come in here and either steal my clothing and stuff or break it. They’re not going to take my memories, too.

Author’s notes: *My grandparents on both sides experienced Alzheimer’s and dementia. I wanted to imagine what it must be like in their heads, going from memory to non-memory states and the resulting confusion for everyone.*

Scheduled for publication in Running Wild Anthology of Short Stories Volume 2.

THE POWER OF PERSUASION

"And how does that make you feel?"

Tony didn't have to think about it much. He had been thinking about it for the past several weeks, ever since he noticed the change in her behavior. "It makes me angry, of course. And hurt."

"Angry," the man sitting in the leather recliner repeated, ignoring the word hurt. "Why?"

"The cues are obvious. The sudden showers after being out 'with the girls,' the sexy underwear she would never wear for me, even when I begged her. I'm not blind…or stupid."

"Stupid, you feel stupid," the man repeated back. "And angry," he added. "How angry? Enough to divorce her?"

"Angry enough to divorce her," he repeated.

"Angry enough to kill her," Tony spoke, more of a statement than a question.

"Angry enough to kill her," the man in the chair affirmed matter-of-factly.

"Cheating on you like that is wrong, after all you have given her. When you see the underwear on the bureau, you picture her with her lover, don't you?"

"I picture her with her lover."

"When you see it, it makes you angry. Angry enough to kill her."

"Angry enough to kill her," Tony repeated back.

The man in the leather chair pushed himself to a standing position. "When you see the sexy underwear, you will see the woman nearest to them as a stuffed animal. It will be safe to choke the animal, because it isn't a living person. You can take out all of your anger on that object. Do you understand?"

"Yes."

"When I snap my fingers, you won't remember this conversation. You will feel relaxed and calm. UNTIL you see the sexy underwear. Then you will get very angry and see a stuffed animal and choke it as hard as you can. Now, wake up," and Dr. Tom snapped his fingers. Tony opened his eyes. "How do you feel, Tony" Dr. Tom asked?

"Relaxed. Good. I always feel better after these sessions," he replied.

"Good. I understand that the wives have arranged for us getting together tonight." Dr. Tom told him. "So I will see you around 7."

"Great. I have to run and finish the office work. See you then." He took Dr. Tom's smaller hand in his and shook it closely.

Some people, like Tony, were easy to put under. Others are more difficult. Dr. Tom was glad that Tony was one of the easy ones, given the affair he was having with Tony's wife Linda. He valued the friendship but he loved Tony's wife more.

The window overlooking the parking lot was convenient. As soon as Dr. Tom saw Tony exit the building, he pressed the speed dial to Tony's home. "OK Linda, the trigger is set. It's the underwear. When he sees it, he'll get angry and the suggestion I implanted will drive him to choke the female closest to him, thinking she is a stuffed animal. That needs to be Mary. He'll see my wife but picture her as the stuffed animal and choke her to death. Then you and I can end all this hiding nonsense." There was silence on the other end. "Linda, are you there?"

"Yes. It's perfect, Love. My brother Chris will be here tonight. He'll be in uniform, just coming off duty. It's soooo perfect."

"YOU are so perfect, Love"

"No, you. Gotta go. See you in a few hours." The dial tone returned.

* * * * *

Dinner had been wonderful. Chris was checking his texts downstairs as Tony and Linda joined Mary and Dr. Tom in the master bathroom to admire the recently installed hot tub. That's when Tony saw the sexy panties and bra Linda had "accidentally" left on the sink side.

Tony stared for a second and then visibly seethed. He moved to Dr. Tom and throttled him. Dr. Tom was taken off guard and his small frame was no match for Tony's workman hands and linebacker size. The women watched and shrieked at Tony to stop.

Chris ran up the stairs, his boots audibly announced his advancement. He yelled at Tony to stop but the big man continued a few more seconds until the audible snap made it clear that it was too late. Dr. Tom slumped to the floor, eyes rolled back into their sockets. Chris easily subdued Tony, forced him to the ground and handcuffed him.

Mary screamed and Linda lay in a crumpled ball crying. Chris used his phone to call for backup and held Tony face down to the floor with his foot.

"He just went berserk. He was our best friend. Why would he do that?"

"I don't know, I am so sorry," Linda said between sobs, holding her friend in a tight grip.

"I need to go to the station but I'll be back," Chris told them before walking Tony downstairs.

From the master bedroom window, they watched Chris and his partner leave with the killer. As the squad car pulled away, the two women rubbed their eyes and sat close to one other on the bed.

"Like it was hard to reprogram the hypnosis," Mary smirked. "Before I left the practice to raise Billy, I was twice the hypnotist he ever was."

"Men are so easy," Linda agreed. "Flash a little skin, make a couple of suggestions, and they'll do anything. Including do themselves in."

Linda ran her fingers lightly through Mary's long hair. "Now they'll both be out of our lives and we can be with who we really want." Linda used Mary's hair to pull her face close. She lightly bit her bottom lip while letting out a small moan. "And you look so hot in the underwear. How about putting them on for me and modeling them. How does it make you feel when you wear them?"

"Totally under your control."

Watch the author read the story:

https://www.youtube.com/watch?v=4p15bYc0IQk&t=144s

Author's notes: *At some point, everyone wants to write a murder mystery. Once again, doing this in flash format is tough, especially if you want to include a twist. In this case, I wanted to try to incorporate a double twist, since people who were reading my work were already expecting a twist of some sort. So, the second twist becomes the real twist.*

This is one of my favorite pieces I have written.

SIXTY MINUTES

I'm dreaming. But even in the dream, I realize it's a dream. I'm standing in an amalgam of my childhood home and my current house. Things I recognize are mixed with those I don't. And it's all in color. I read somewhere that people don't dream in color. It may be muted but it's definitely color.

My dad is sitting on the green sofa that my mom bought in the early 1970s. It's the fifth dream of him this month. My last dream was that he had moved away, not telling anyone where he went. I somehow knew he started a new life in another state working as a staff accountant. It's hard to understand since he owned his own accounting firm. Despite begging and pleading for him to return contact, he wouldn't. I spent the whole dream trying to understand his new life and why he left. It was perpetual heartache.

But today, here he is: sitting on the sofa and smiling. Despite it being an amalgam of the homes I've lived in, I recognize it as his home. He stays seated as I speak to him.

"I'm so glad you're here."

"Actually, *you* are here," he corrects me and laughs like he just told one of his old, often repeated jokes. It makes me smile. Then, I remember that he's dead. Dad died two months ago in a traffic accident. There were no chances for last goodbyes; he was gone before I could reach him. It simultaneously seems like yesterday and a year ago. His appearance here confuses me but makes me happy. I don't say anything about my confusion or his death, afraid that he may suddenly disappear if I do.

He pats the sofa cushion next to him. "Sit down on the couch and let's talk."

So I sit. It turns out that I do most of the talking. My heart is filled with happiness. I tell him how much I love him and miss him. "Seth and I have been looking at old family photo albums, even the ones from before he was born. He's a good kid but it takes a lot of energy to keep up with him." I pause. "I think *you* taught me how to be a good father." His smile grows bigger at my comment.

"I like this. It makes me feel good. So will you keep coming to my dreams?"

He is quiet and the non-response gives me the answer I dread. "We get an hour. It's a gift to us and the people we love. But just one hour."

It seems amazingly generous and cruel at the same time. It's not nearly enough time. I want more. "That means you'll be going away again?" My sense of loss returns even deeper. He just nods but with a funny smile on his face. I don't know what it means. "Why don't Steve and Penny dream of you? When I ask them, they tell me that they never dream of you."

"Because you need me the most. I gave my sixty minutes to you." I know that he's right. They didn't...don't love him any less. But for some reason, their grief seems less intense. Mine feels crushing and unbearable. I feel selfish and start to cry. I can feel the wetness of the tears roll down my cheeks and taste them in the corners of my mouth. My heart grows incredibly heavy and my throat tightens so that I can't speak. He answers my unvoiced question.

"There are rules with the sixty minutes. I can't control the dream. I can appear but *your* mind guides it. Sometimes I can push it a little in this direction or that." It made sense, in a way, but did that mean this was his conversation with me or mine with him? I probably would never know.

"You may dream of me later but that will be all you and not really me." I want to ask him more questions, about why some people are ghosts, whether reincarnation is real, and whether our destinies are open or set. We never get to those answers but he answers the question that I least wanted an answer to. "This is my last time. And I have to go."

He stands and I follow. He holds out his arms and we hug tightly. I can feel the warmth of his arms on my body and he strokes my hair like I do to my son Seth when I hug him. I'm teary but comforted.

"The secret is creating memories for each other, over and over." Scenes flash through my head at lightning speed: I'm four with the two of us in Halloween costumes; six with him holding the back of my new two-wheeler without training wheels for the first time; nine in a deli eating breakfast on vacation; fourteen with him by the roadside changing a flat; twenty two with him in the audience of my college graduation; thirty and visiting the first house I bought, and so many more. Memories with my Dad are rich and plentiful. "Memories outlast everything else."

He is almost through the doorway but turns to add one last thing… "Don't waste your time focused on what you can't do. Figure out what you *can* do. And have faith. I may not be in your dreams but I AM watching over you. Every day." Then he walked out and I woke up. My pillow was wet and my eyes stung.

And I have a little more faith in what I can make happen today. I have to. Because I know he's watching.

Author's notes: *While this wasn't my exact dream, I am the only one in my family that was dreaming of my father. I wondered why, but really, it wasn't hard to guess. I needed him in my dreams more than anyone else did.*

This is the second story I wrote about my father in my dreams. I generally don't want to repeat exact themes but this one seemed to better express my thoughts on the topic, so I continued it to its finish.

SUN BLOCK

"Better protect that thing or you'll be sorry later," she looked me in the eye while pointing at my boy parts, which just happened to be pointing back at her. She said it matter-of-factly as though she were referring to my nose or shoulders or my feet. But she wasn't.

"I did, already, but I guess it could use another shot," I replied without a trace of acknowledgement of the double meaning in my words.

"Here, use mine," she offered and handed me her SPF 50 spray bottle. There's a certain set of rules to follow on a nude beach and I was just learning them, this being my first visit. You shouldn't stare for too long at other people. You can't have sex on the beach or in the ocean. You can't touch another person's genitals in a sexual way. I am pretty sure that hand-spreading cream into my pubic area fell into at least one of those categories. So I sprayed myself a bit. She looked at me. "You better rub that in or you will look like a leopard," she offered without even a crack of a smile.

"Is that allowed?"

"I think so. You'll be in a lot of trouble if you don't. I had a cousin who…" but she interrupted herself mid-sentence. "You better just do it."

I started rubbing myself in front of her and everyone within eyeshot. She giggled an innocent giggle.

"That's better, right?"

I didn't look down at my affected area. "Yeah, I guess so."

Other people, mostly men were circling the area like sharks stalking their protected prey: my new beach friend. They didn't say anything; just walked close, looking in our direction. Then standing there, they looked away at the ocean or a non-existent object down the beach.

I looked at each as competition and quickly sized them up. That guy has a jungle growth of pubic hair. Good Lord, spend a little time grooming, you bear. A woman could lose her entire hand in there. Okay, geezer with man-boobs. No competition for me except maybe for grannies who have humped their late husband to death. And you, boy-o, get real. You're probably just five years older than her son. Not every woman is a cougar.

A few were too studly to have physical flaws, so I assigned them some non-visual ones. Homer is an eighth-grade drop-out. Vinnie speaks with a stupid-sounding jersey accent. Horace has early onset of diabetes that prevents him from achieving an erection. Keep watching while I am the one talking with her.

We talked about her home town and mine; about personalities at work and about her passions as an artist. It was a real conversation but the entire time we are talking, I can't help wondering "what is she really thinking?" I am standing here with my boy parts pointing at her girl parts in front of all these people pretending not to stare at us. I am (so far) resisting the urge to touch myself or touch her. I'm looking for a clue, a signal, anything to tell me that this is more than a conversation about home towns and art.

The sun starts to set and people start leaving the beach. They roll up the blankets, fold up their chairs and put on cover-ups, to walk the path through the dunes, back to their cars in the parking lot. The flies are biting. We swat at just a few at first, but it becomes distracting. "The flies aren't the only ones that are hungry. So am I. How about you?" I ask, thinking this kind of clever transition separates me from the others.

"Yeah a bit. I know a place nearby." She pulls her shorts up and over her slim hips and a tank top down over her head. Like a thirteen year old boy getting his first accidental glance at a real live naked woman, I've memorized her every curve. I help carry her things to her car and we drive off in search of dinner where I hope to ply her with a little wine and get her back out of her pants. As we eat, we chat like old friends.

As she finished the last of her wine, the time was right. "So how about we go back to my place and we continue..." I paused before completing my sentence "or maybe you would be more comfortable at your place?"

She took the glass from her lips and placed it on the table. "I am not sure I know you well enough for that." I was dumbfounded. I had spent the better part of an hour talking to her, stark naked in various states of arousal. Then I spent two hours at dinner, clothed. She recognized the confusion on my face and continued. "I like being seen naked."

"I like you being naked, too. So I would be glad to see you that way again."

"It's different on the beach. It's less and more sexual with all of those people. It makes me hot, excited."

"Me, too," I mumbled.

"And so does doing nothing about it. That makes me the hottest of all. That I am there on display. And that people can't touch me, not because I won't let them but for some other reason. A reason neither of us can control. The rules."

"So what makes you hottest is NOT having sex? Not touching?"

"Exactly. Look, I need to go." She stood up and her top showed off her shape. She started to leave and then turned around to look me in the eye. "I'll be back on the beach next Saturday. Feel free to look me up...and down." She smiled, turned and left.

I stood up and my pants rubbed against my boy parts. It hurt. Damn sunburn.

It turns out that SPF 50, although the highest protection they make, isn't near enough to protect you from getting burned on the beach.

Author's notes: *A naked beach is such a guy fantasy…until we get there. Should we stare? Will everyone look at me? What happens when we react to what we see? I want to look big but maybe I don't want to look too big, if you know what I mean…*

TERRORISM

It starts, as it always does, with one man. A small group of others gather around him to make plans. It's the conversation no one outside the room is supposed to hear.

"The room is secure?"

"Absolutely."

"Because what we are speaking about here…"

"It's secure."

"So what are we looking for at an event?" an aid questions.

"An explosion," another answers.

"An explosion of action."

"Terror the likes of which the western world has seldom seen," said a third.

"Terror, my friends," the older man lectures, "terror places us in control. Do this right, the explosion comes hard. It comes fast. We destroy lives, but only for the greater good. It will solidify our power. And the truth is, only the undeserving will fall. Our great country will become great once again.

After we start this, they will always be looking over their shoulders, wondering…is he one, is she one? They will be running around chasing their tails while we…..while we take the ultimate power."

"All that misdirection and then we make our power play?"

"Absolutely, the self-important will fall. Terror is power. We will be the power. We will be in control." He raised his fist in the air. The others followed his lead.

"Now let's start this." Stepping from his entourage, he walked from the meeting room and out onto the platform.

"I have here in my hand a list of 205—a list of names that were made known to the Secretary of State as being members of the Communist Party and who nevertheless are still working and shaping policy in the State Department," Senator McCarthy addressed the Republican Women's Club of Wheeling, West Virginia.

And on February 9, 1950, the world fell into chaos just as planned.

Author's notes: *One of my shorter pieces. I don't talk a lot about politics because, honestly, who really wants to hear what I have to say about it? But I think this says a whole lot about my thoughts on politics in general.*

TOPSY TURVY

The Brentworth's party was a sea of black tuxes accompanying little black or red cocktail dresses highlighting, *for the most part*, just the right amount of cleavage and leg. A short, stocky man with Fred Flintstone face-stubble, a bad comb-over and a fat stogy between his fingers approached to tell me about *the other part.*

"I just saw your wife flash before my eyes."

"You mean you saw *your life* flash before your eyes?"

"No. Your wife. Flash. You know, lift her top and jiggle her goodies." He cupped his thick, hairy hands to jiggle large invisible breasts in front of him.

Time to go find her. She only does it at parties of well-to-do society types AFTER cosmopolitans. I'm pretty sure they feed her the drinks. Now, a dozen or so guys seek me out, slap me on the shoulder and make comments on the gravity-defying nature of her breasts. The women will silently walk past me, giving dirty looks…and not the good kind.

"Where is she now?"

"Down by the punch bowl. Quite a line of guys. I just thought you should know."

"Thanks. I'll go save her from herself."

"Just look for the crowd," he half-yelled over the din.

Her tendency to flash after drinking keeps our social calendar pretty full. We don't accept ALL of the invitations…no one could. I assume that I'm viewed as her designated driver: if they could address the invitation to her alone, they probably would. Nobody really cares where I go or who I speak with at these things; most of the time they're just as happy when I can't be easily found.

When I enter the room, her top is mostly back in place. The circle of people surrounding her opens for me with mixed looks of guilt and smugness. I put my arm around her. "Had a bit to drink?" I ask her.

"Not that mush," she slurred loudly and finds the spot beneath my arm. Everyone is looking at me. I should be more embarrassed than I am. I wrap my jacket around her while handing her empty cosmo glass to whichever gawker is standing closest to me.

"Need any help?" a voice offered.

"No, I can get her to the car fine. We're going to call it a night."

Out in the rush of the cool air and away from the crowd, she sobers up quickly. "So what did they say?"

"About what?"

"About me, silly. My performance."

"A lot of the usual. You seemed very happy. How you light up the party. What a perfect rack you have."

"All natural, too. That gym membership has really paid off. Two guys offered to take me outside but you know I am never THAT intoxicated. With their eyes focused on one…well, two things…you know that it's elementary slight of hand. They think I've downed a half dozen drinks."

"One of the benefits of being a former magician's assistant," I laughed. "And all of that attention on what YOU are doing means that people don't want to find me right away. They want to see how far they can get you to go."

"Or go WITH me. Even the women. Some of them like it even better than the men. They wish that they could command the attention."

"I am sure that's true from a psychological perspective. I just read a paper from Harvard Medical School that was exploring the concept that…"

"Enough of that psychobabble. You know what I want to know."

"Really?" I teased. "The paper was quite…revealing."

She smiled, showing her perfectly straight and white teeth. "Tell me."

"Two platinum and diamond bracelets. A pair of earrings. And Alison Brentworth's ruby and diamond necklace you have always admired."

"Oh, I want to keep that one. Just for a little while. Please?"

"You know the rules."

"Okay," she sighed.

"This is so much better than scaling the roofs and working on those alarm systems in the middle of the night. We can be in bed and asleep by one AM."

"YOU were right. How many times do I have to tell you that?"

"Two more times…this month."

"When they eventually discover the things missing from the safe, they'll never connect it to the party or us."

"I think we'll be getting an invitation from the Kleinfeld's for their party next month. He was quite taken with you tonight."

"And he'll be quite taken, also," she laughed. "I should wear something special. Mind if I take a couple of hundred to go find an appropriate red gown?"

"Fine. But don't go crazy. They're much more interested in what will be coming out of it."

"What will we do when these things drop to my waist?" She cupped them in her hands and let them fall. "I hate the idea of surgery."

"By then, Jimmy and Joanie will have graduated med or law school. You could always become a nurse and take things from retirement homes while the old folks sleep. But leave them their teeth…and their dignity."

"Maybe I'll just steal all the stuff back from you…"

"What have I got for you to steal? You've already stolen my heart."

She wrapped her arm around me and pulled me into her. She touched her lips to mine and I felt the slippery gloss of her very red lipstick. Her tongue lightly touched the bottom of my upper lip and then she lightly bit me. My heart jumped like it always does when she kisses me. "You are the prefect man," she whispered.

"I am," I nodded, and started walking again. "But put the necklace back in my pocket. I felt you slide it out. You are seriously out of practice. I was wrong. I don't think you could even take that retirement home job."

"*Almost* perfect man," she sighed and she wedged the jewelry back into my pocket.

I held the car door open and lightly swatted her ass as she climbed in. "Can't bullshit a bullshitter."

Author's notes: *Another situation where I used the same concept twice: Can I take a woman flashing her breasts and make it a legitimate story?*

I remember walking down the street in West Chester borough and trying to think of the most outrageous concept for a story, and if I could work my way out of it.

The last line may be common to most people: my introduction to it came from the parent of one of my high school friends.

WEDDING JITTERS

She slapped him hard in the face. The resulting sound was loud: loud enough that even as an observer, I winced. The timing was unfortunately perfect since the band had just finished playing their song. Silence followed. Not a whimper from him, not a curse word from her, and not a whisper from anyone else. She quickly spun around, her dress swaying like a princess' gown. The clopping from her high heels started loud and faded as she exited at the far side of the room, as though the spontaneous event was planned for the most dramatic exit possible. The whispers start and the crown gets louder.

And I wonder…what caused the slap? What suddenly happened between the bride's maid and the best man? Is this the first time she slapped him or the 10th…or the 100th? I go to the bar and order two drinks, then head through the doorway into the adjacent room. She's sitting in the chair looking out the window.

"So, hi. You look like you might appreciate a drink," and I hand her a glass. She doesn't ask what's in it. She takes and swallows the contents in two gulps.

"Thanks," she offers in a monotone and turns her gaze

back to the window.

"So, what a party, huh? I mean, great entertainment. The band is awesome and some guy just about got his head slapped off by a gorgeous girl who makes the bride look like bride of Frankenstein. Makes you wonder what that poor shmuck must have said or done. Did you see it?"

She turned to me and stared me down with that same look she gave the guy after slapping him. I wasn't sure whether to prepare for my own face slapping. Her stare softened and she started laughing.

"I guess everyone saw, huh?" she said.

"Pretty much."

"Are they talking about it?"

"A little. You know, maid of honor takes a whack at the best man. It adds intrigue to the whole wedding thing."

"I guess it would," she smiled. "I'm Tori," she extended her arm and offered me her hand. "And you are?"

"A guy who wants to watch your hand very carefully." We both laughed. "Walt."

"No last name, Walt?"

"I'm saving it for a lull in the conversation."

"Hmmm," she murmured and the lull presented itself.

"Simone."

"Hello, Walt Simone."

"So what made you slap him?" I asked.

"I was wondering when you would get around to asking me that."
"Was it something he said?"

"Did you think it was?"

"It seemed like it could have been."

"Then let's say it was."

"That's hardly an answer."

"You want to know the truth?" she asked.

"Or some fantastic fiction that I can tell at future weddings."

"Is the wedding over?" she questioned.

"Not completely. Some people are heading out, but the band is still playing."

"Whose side invited you?"

"The bride's."

"Okay Walter Simone, asker-of-questions. It was not something he said. It was a cover-up"

"What kind of cover-up?"

"The kind to protect a friend. A good friend."

"Now it gets interesting. So how does slapping a guy in public protect a friend?"

"I walked in on *her* in the bathroom.... with an old friend."

The way she said her, it was obvious that *her* was the bride.

"Ah, a little prenuptial nuptials. Weddings bring out the romance in people…sometimes even the bride."

"Exactly. People might've seen them entering the room together and so I created a…small diversion."

"Interesting definition of small."

"Smaller than the alternative."

"Did he know? That he was part of a diversion?"

"Not exactly. I probably owe him an apology. I'll text him later."

"Good idea. If he sees you coming, he probably won't hang around to talk," I laughed. "Why him?"

"He was nearby. I met him at the practice dinner and he came to the wedding alone."

"How considerate of you, not to embarrass someone who had a date."

"I'm a giving person," she smiled again. "It may help him score with the bride's slut cousin Robin." She reached over and took my drink from my hand and began sipping it."

"Given your description of her, he may not have needed the help. The bride do that a lot?"

"Can't say."

"*Can't* say or *won't* say."

"You're a smart boy. Friends keep secrets or they don't get to keep secrets…or be friends"

"So…if you are good at keeping secrets, why tell me this one?"

"I never named *her*, you did. And you look trustworthy. Or maybe because you were the only one who came to see how I was."

"Suppose it was just to find out why it happened."

She stared me in the eye again. "I read people pretty well. You wanted that, too. But that isn't why you came to me. You've been looking at me all night. You think girls don't notice? We do. It doesn't mean we'll make it easier for you, just because we know. That's part of the testing."

"The testing?"

"Yes, to see if you have the balls to follow through on what you're thinking. A girl doesn't want a guy who can't follow through."

She's confident and fearless, beautiful and smart. There's just one thing to do. I stand up and point to the door. "Let's go for a dance. I'd like to end the evening dancing with you."

"*Maybe* it won't be the end."

"Maybe not." I hold my hand out and she takes it. I hold her hand firmly and give it a squeeze. "I just want to make sure I'm not the object of another distraction."

"Oh honey, I have a much different distraction planned for you…if you know how to dance."

Author's notes: *Many of my stories show the guy as inept and easily manipulated by women. In this case, I wanted to still keep the female as a strong character but not characterize the guy as I had before.*

One of my favorite movies, "My Favorite Year," features one character creating a diversion so that another character can take the girl away from her date. I wanted to change it up a bit but use that concept to tell a different "boy and girl" story.

WAITING

"Why do guys die first?" my friend Bob asks the new guy sitting on the bench.

New Guy looks up and squints because the light is silhouetting Bob's and my standing figures from behind, probably offering a halo effect. "I don't know. Why?"

"Because they want to," Bob laughs. There's a moment of silence as New Guy looks to his left and right. With no one in sight, he laughs hard, as if he had been told the funniest joke ever. I laugh, too. It could be the fiftieth time Bob has told the joke but I still laugh every time. Then they exchange a silent look, as though they share a secret.

"Beautiful view from here," New Guy commented.

Bob nodded. "Been here long?"

"No I just got here last week."

"The wife?"

"I need to check the schedule. Soon I expect."

"Well, unless she makes a detour to play with old Henry," Bob smirked.

New guy held a serious look for a second, then burst out laughing again. "We don't know a Henry."

Bob stared New Guy in the eyes. "Everyone knows a Henry. Sometimes his name is actually Henry. Sometimes it's Fred or Tim or Francois. I hate when they have French names."

"I don't think so. She's not like that."

"You never know. That's the one problem leaving women alone. There's always a Henry. There was a point when I was a Henry. I remember me and the women from the club when the husbands were out working and ogling their secretaries. Ooh la la."

"I don't believe I have anything to worry about." New Guy's tone turned terse.

"Stop goading him," I finally spoke up and chastised Bob in an attempt to diffuse the tension. He was a good friend but sometimes didn't know where to draw the line.

"So whatcha gonna do today?" I asked Bob, redirecting the conversation.

"The same thing I get to do every day. Smoke some cigars, play some golf. The landscaping on the course is really heavenly." Bob smiled, clearly pleased with himself. "Wanna join?" he directed to New Guy.

"I really never played," New Guy offered.

"Not a problem," Bob said. "We can teach you. You might get good before the wife rejoins you."

"It *would* fill the time. When are you expecting yours back? How long do you have?"

"Five years, two months and four days," Bob smiled. "I checked the schedule." Then, unexpectedly, a sudden sadness overcame him. The smile slid from his face as he looked down. His body slumped as he lightly kicked at the air.

"You can play a lot of golf in that time." New Guy offered.

Bob lifted his head and a smaller smile returned to his face. "Yep. Plan to."

"Ok I'm game." New Guy stood up. "Which way to the course?"

"To the left, past the second fluffy cloud."

Author's notes: *The opening line "Why do men die before women?" is an old joke I heard and would retell at times I was…annoyed.*

The first version of the story wasn't softened and I realized after placing it away for a short while that what I really needed to show was that despite the joke, the men missed their female counterparts. It became a much better "story" when the joke was counterbalanced by the sense of the men being lost without their mates.

Originally published on the EverdayFiction.com website.

THE NAKED TRUTH

The BING from my phone alerted me to the receipt of a new text. I opened it and was greeted by a well-lit photo of a large set of breasts with pointy nipples, pushed upward by a set of hands with sparkly purple polished fingernails. I didn't recognize the breasts or the hands but was certainly grateful that someone thought enough of me to send me the picture.

I angled the phone so that the person sitting next to me to my right couldn't see the screen: a large set of naked tits often disturbs a business meeting. As I admired them, the question remained: whose were these? The phone number was unfamiliar with no reference in my address book. I faked a coughing jag where people showed genuine concern for my welfare and excused myself for a break.

What's the proper protocol in the case of receiving an unsolicited naked selfie? Do you send a thank you text? Do you send a return photo? Do you ask who the person is? While pondering these questions, I returned to my office and shut the door behind me. I needed to think.

My phone binged once again. This time, it was the photo of a particularly fine round ass in boy shorts. I don't honestly know why or how people could actually call them boy shorts as they are most definitely on a woman's ass. I enlarged the picture for a better look. No identifying marks I recognized: this was not an ass I knew. I wasn't not sure whether to be disappointed or elated.

A third bing and I'm like Pavlov's dog. This time just two question marks.

"Thank you," I tapped back.

"And?" appeared quickly in response.

"Nice to see you." I still had no idea who it is.

"U?"

I hate when people abbreviate in texts. It looks so…uneducated. Then again, I was willing to make an allowance given when they send me outstanding body parts photos. Ok, now I have to make a choice. I play it vague. "More?"

"U first."

It could be a girl I met the other night and slipped my number. I could have been wrong when I thought I saw her drop it in her half-drank beer. And my friend's wife was flirting pretty heavily with me at the party last week. She would know my cell phone number or have asked her hubby for it. Maybe it was the girl from the sales call a week ago. I was pretty sure that she gave me the twice-over.

Whoever it was, this person has already taken a risk with me, sending me some sexy pics. My office door is closed. No one can see in. I switch the camera to the one that faces me. I swallow deep.

Swoosh. The file is sent over the airwaves to my new friend. I hope she likes it.

“Haha. Nice balls...” Ball, technically. It’s a picture of my eyeball. But whoever it was got my joke. Another bing. “Show more.”

I took a deep breath and walked into the men’s room, locked the door, turned on the light and face the mirror above the sink. My pants and underwear drop to the ground. Suddenly, I scramble to check that there’s nobody already in the stall, then return to the mirror. I suck in my belly that is as much as I can and frame the shot so I carefully hide my face. I snap a couple pictures. Small bings indicate that the pictures being stored on the phone. I make a mental note that I will have to erase them after I use them.

Then I reviewed them. Not bad for a middle aged guy. I hit the send button. And wait.

It's two full minutes and I am thinking what? Am I ugly? Were they too explicit? She asked me for the pics. Is she posting them on some public sex offender web site? I started to sweat and my knees got weak.

Then came the bing.

“Nice. Very nice. You’re a big boy.”

Does she mean my belly or something else? I decide not to ask, but pose a different question. "How about something from you below the equator?"

I head a bing and open the email. "We should meet later." It's accompanied by a couple more shots. First a beautiful ass shot in sexy thong. Then a side view and then…a front view of the same person who is apparently hung better than I am. Yikes. Apparently, my new friend isn't the most beautiful girl I have ever seen. I've just texted my goodies to someone who knows me, that I don't know, who is a better man than I am.

Bing. Another text. "Should I come to your place?" Crap, does this person know where my place is? Do they know me? I panic.

I freeze for a moment and do what any person who put themselves in this position would do. I lie. Tap tap tap.

"I found the phone and decided to have some fun before I return it to the owner. Thanks for the pics. Mind if I post them?"

"I prefer you don't. Wanna meet anyway? I am probably just minutes away."

Crap crap crap.

I drop the phone on the floor and smash my heel into my cell phone, cracking the screen and then the casing. It was time for an upgrade anyway. I'd get one of the newer phones that has more features…and is visibly larger so that if I encounter my friend, he/she sees the difference and asks about my missing phone.

I pick up the damaged phone, slip it into my pants pocket and walk back to my desk. I go without it for the day, then buy the new one. I was due for an upgrade anyway. I think.

Although I am still wondering who sent me the pics. They *were* awfully nice breasts.

Author's notes: *I was very tentative writing this story. I liked the concept of revealing pictures being accidentally sent and received. This story could be told a hundred different ways. I definitely like writing stories on sexy situations that don't actually involve sex. But I had a lot of trouble figuring out a good payoff for the end.*

So a friend read it and made the suggestion that it be a guy instead of a girl, which seemed perfect. After that, it was easy to flesh it out. Sometimes, important parts of a story come from outside inspiration instead of my own.

Again, I was reluctant to share this with my writers group, but there was a month that I didn't have anything else to bring. They liked it but at this point probably think I am a total perv.

GAMES PEOPLE PLAY

It generally takes two or three glasses of wine before I can get a new girl comfortable enough that I can suggest "The Game."

I chose *'Orange Nails'* because she had a crunchy look: long wild wavy hair, big hoop earrings, peasant skirt. And those open-toed sandals with orange nail polish. Orange: it's just a color you don't see often in conservative circles. The ones that march to their own drum are the most interesting in bed. It was clear that Orange Nails was the right choice.

"Let's play 'Name A State'," I suggested at my regular back-of-the-bar table.

"Okay," she said. "That sounds fun. I know my states."

I smiled. "Name a state that starts with 'A'." I looked into her eyes, opening my own just slightly wider after placing my hand on her knee.

"Arizona," she replied after a brief pause.

"No, Alabama, where men are men and dogs run scared" and I moved my hand two inches up her thigh. "Name a state that starts with 'S'."

Her eyes got just a bit wider. The maroon table cloth fell low enough that they covered her thigh and my hand from view, but even so, her eyes darted around the room to see if others noticed. No one was looking at us. "South Carolina?"

"Sorry, no. South Dakota, where all the guys cheer 'Go South'." I slid my hand another couple of inches to midway up her thigh. Despite having done the same just seconds before, she once again scanned the room. I could almost see her mentally calculating the number of states left before my hand reached directly between her thighs.

She gave the smallest smile before asking me the question. "How do I know that you aren't changing the answer at the last second?"

"Yeah, how DO you know that?" I mocked her and gazed into her eyes. "I guess you have to trust me. Do you trust me?"

"Well given that this is our FIRST time together, I don't know. Should I?"

"I think you should. I haven't lied about much so far…nothing important anyway. A little about my height, my weight, my age, my income..."

"You lied about your age?"

"Well, now that you ask me directly, yeah. But don't worry, I can't get arrested for under-age drinking and I haven't gotten an application for my AARP card yet, so, I think it's all good. Round three, it's the big event. Are you ready?"

"Do I have a choice?" She stared into my eyes.

"Sure. You could stand up..."

She looked down to the table and then back at me. "I'm interested to see where this goes."

"I think we both know where this goes. The question is how fast it gets there and whether it encounters any obstructions."

"Like the sudden appearance of a fork?" She toyed with me.

"I was thinking of something a little less sharp. Besides, you might miss and stab yourself."

"That would be an unintended consequence. What would you suggest?"

"I do know another game." I pulled my hand from her thigh.

"For some reason, I'm not surprised."

"It's a play-at-home version. You have to sign a waiver in advance."

"A waiver? Is the game dangerous?"

"Not so much dangerous as un-pre-dic-table." I enunciated the last syllables more heavily.

"Do tell," she encouraged.

"It's called 'Name The Household Object'. We go to your place so they are objects you're already familiar with."

"You point at things and I name them? That doesn't seem very fun or challenging," she pouted. "Especially after the 'Name The State' game."

"I agree. So I added a trick to it. The guesser is blindfolded. He or SHE needs to name the object by touch."

"That's a little more interesting, although that doesn't sound too difficult, either."

"Oh…did I mention that you can't touch it with your hands?"

"No. You neglected to mention that."

"Oh, well, that becomes obvious after your arms are tied together above your head."

She pursed her lips and wrinkled her forehead. "That doesn't sound comfortable."

"It's okay, you're naked, so your clothes don't bunch up. I just touch the objects to your different body parts to see how long it takes you to identify them."

"How long do I get?"

"Longer than average." I smiled widely at the double meaning.

She stared at me, squinting her eyes. "How long is longer than average?" she plays along.

"Pretty long. And you get as much time as you need or like. Some objects you just want to make really sure before you make your guess."

"Hmmmmmm." She paused and her eyes looked to the side, as if she were imagining an object right then. She focused back on me. "Have you played this game a lot?"

"No. Sadly. Most of the women I know don't like games. They don't even like the 'Name The State' game. Not very adventurous."

"So I am in your top ten?"

"You could be in my top one."

She grabbed her phone from her purse and tapped in a message. It dinged a few seconds later. "Turns out my roomie is out for the evening. And I like the top," she smiled slightly. "I'll play."

* * * * * *

Her place was a small walkup apartment several minutes away on the third floor above a Chinese restaurant. As we climbed the stairs, my eyes followed the sway of her ass in the peasant skirt trying to see whether she was wearing a thong or any underwear at all. The light in the hallway was too dim to tell but I was confident that I would know soon enough.

I sat on the arm of the couch while poured us drinks.

"Do you actually need a signed waiver?" she asked.

"I can accept something orally, if you prefer." She looked puzzled at first and then laughed. "You're funny," she said and I had to agree.

"So you want to play?"

"I have an idea. Maybe you should show me how the game is played."

"Aren't I showing you right now?"

"Not exactly. Maybe YOU should be on the bed and try to guess the objects."

"I guess I could do that."

"OK I'm going to change into something less restricting. You get in that same 'naked' state and lie on the bed. Then we'll touch you with objects and see which ones you can guess. Guess three and I take off the blindfold."

"Three? That seems fair."

"No cheating. Blindfold on when I come out."

This girl was fun. I liked her. A lot.

Her bed had a pink and purple flowered comforter. I pulled it down, slipped out of my clothes and into the blindfold. A minute later I heard the squeak of what I assumed was the bathroom door and suddenly felt her presence above me. She made sure the blindfold was secure before speaking.

"You said the rule was no looking and no hands, right?"

"Right," I smiled.

"What guarantee do I have that you'll follow your own rules?

"My word is my bond." I said

"I need a better guarantee than that, sir." I could almost hear the smile in her voice. "Suppose I just loosely tie your wrists together with these scarves?"

I was about to protest when I felt the scarf wrap my wrists. She gently raised my hands above my head. "You are on your honor to leave your arms in that position."

"I am nothing if not honorable."

"Okay, honey." Her voice as sweet as her name for me. "Let's see if I understand how we play this game. Here's number one." There was a void of any sound and then I heard a buzzing followed by a vibration on my thigh. She ran it up and down each thigh. I jumped a little but left my hands above my head. "Can you guess?"

"I think I know but try a more sensitive spot on my body. My thighs have never been the most sensitive."

The vibration point moved, and I felt it along my sides and hips. It felt good.

"What is it," she whispered an inch from my ear.

"Your vibrator?" I love girls that use toys. It means they are all about pleasure.

"Good boy." The buzzing stopped and I was a little disappointed. But the disappointment was only momentary.

"Here's the second." I felt a soft, wet feeling swipe down my neck and to my left nipple. It danced around it and then ran to my right nipple. She was skilled as I couldn't feel any other part of her body touching me at the same time.

"I can't be sure," I grinned and hesitated. "Could you do it again?"

"Okay," came the reply and I felt her trace the same line, and I felt my nipple harden.

"T-t-t" I stuttered on purpose. "It feels like a….." and as my body arched, I realized for the first time that the scarf wasn't *just* tied around my wrists. It was also secured to something above my head. I grunted. Her mouth left my nipple as a hand touched my chest and pressed me back down against the mattress.

"I told you that I have to trust you," she whispered. "You WANT me to trust you, don't you?"

"Yes," was all I could manage.

"Good boy," she took her hand away. There was a long pause.

"What about number three?" My question was immediately followed by three stinging slaps against my thigh. I howled from the unexpected pain. Then silence followed by three more slap sounds and the same harsh stings. I howled again and tried to pull my arms down to protect the area, forgetting that I couldn't.

"Honey," she said, her voice a sweet contrast to the sting, "do you know what that is?"

"A shock. A smack. Something hard."

She pulled the blindfold from me and it took three long seconds for my eyes to focus. Orange Nails was in leather from head to toe with a leather whip in her hands. Standing next to her was a man the size of a linebacker, also clad in black leather but in a full leather face mask with holes for only his eyes and mouth.

"Oh honey. You got the last one wrong. It's your new favorite game. Oh and it turns out my roommate was home after all. Surprise."

Author's notes: *The Name-A-State game is real, one a girl in college introduced to me – although it didn't go very far back then. And 'Orange Nails' was an ironic choice. The day after I finished this, I met a girl at the business next to where I worked that had her nails painted orange. I stared at them and her for a while. It was like a sign.*

BANK NOTES

Emily saw him approach through the bank's glass walls and blushed when the handsome, well-dressed client took his turn in front of her. She noticed that since he began coming to the bank in the beginning of the month, he would wait in her line even when other tellers were available. He wasn't the only one who did that but he WAS the most regular: Fridays at 6:45 pm just before closing, always to make a cash withdrawal from his account. He was the kind of man that would make *any* woman blush. "Good afternoon, sir."

"Good afternoon, Emily," he responded and smiled. His perfect white teeth matched his perfectly tailored suit and perfectly shined shoes. As he passed the withdrawal slip to Emily, his smile never diminished. "I've had my eye on you for a while now," he explained. "There's a note on the back of this…*just for you,*" he whispered the last part so that only she could hear. He squinted slightly; his face and voice went suddenly serious. "DON'T let anyone else see it." Her face went ashen.

She didn't need to read the note: the bank spent days of training to prepare tellers for the most common bank robbery scenarios. This was one of them. Thieves most often used notes on the back of bank withdrawal slips taken from the bank's check writing desk to make the transaction less suspicious to those around them. She thought about the alerts she had read that very morning on the uncaptured gentleman bandit who had robbed three banks in as many weeks in the area. Always polite, he set up a false account in advance and came in a few times to case the bank and target an individual teller before actually robbing the branches. He hadn't killed anyone…yet.

The underside of the slip with the message would be evidence, with his fingerprints intact if she didn't handle it. Without touching the slip, she reached her foot forward, tapping the silent alarm which notified the local police station several blocks away.

Time was a critical element in a robbery. In practice, they could be at the bank in three and a half minutes. Her job, she knew, was twofold – put no one in danger and slip the dye pack bundle of bills into whatever she gave him. The ultrasonic signal at the door would explode red dye all over the bills and whatever was nearby, including him, only after he exited the bank.

"Where is that million-dollar smile I've always seen?" he asked.

"The drawer only holds five thousand," she replied stiffly.

"Then we'll have to go with that, I guess," he laughed. "I AM on a schedule and the branch is about to close." He smiled as though he told a joke nobody else would understand. She did. Following a robbery, the branch would close down. Because banks hold Federal insurance, bank robbery is a federal offense and the FBI would be involved. She would be stuck here for hours and the branch might remain closed for days.

Her directive was to give any thief what he wanted and let him leave. No heroics: the police will catch him outside of the branch office. 99% of all bank robbers are captured eventually.

"You didn't read the note," he moved his eyes from the untouched slip back to her.

"I have a pretty good idea what it says. You've been pretty obvious with what you wanted." He appeared surprised for just a second, then regained his composure. She handed him three envelopes stuffed with bills.

"I hadn't thought I was that obvious," he looked at the envelopes and then back to her. "You must have had only small bills left in your drawer today. No matter, they spend the same. I'm thinking Pescatore's for dinner?" He paused before asking her "Will you be joining me?" His face softened.

His glibness about deciding where to have dinner following his bank robbery felt even creepier. However handsome and charming he was, he was still a thief. And he had targeted *her*. She was angry but held her composure.

"Not tonight. I have a feeling I will have to stay late." His smile disappeared again and he stared into her eyes. "I suppose I could kidnap you." She physically stepped back from the teller station, fearing the worst possible outcome, until his smile reappeared. "No, a gentleman never forces himself on a lady. Have a nice evening," and he turned to walk out the door.

His walk had the same casual swagger as when he walked in the bank. If he weren't a thief… well, it didn't matter. He was. Emily looked around and saw that no one else was aware of what had happened, and what had almost happened. As he exited the bank, she locked off the entry doors remotely as she watched his movements through the glass walls that made up the building.

The dye pack went off as expected, bursting a cloud of red ink around him. As he staggered, four police officers came from the sides of the building and surrounded him. They kicked him to the ground and quickly cuffed him, searching for weapons. Then they pushed him into the squad car and drove away.

A detective entered the bank, following procedure. He secured the bank and Emily's teller station. They dusted for fingerprints before touching anything, including the unmoved withdrawal ticket that had served as the robbery note. Using tweezers, the detective carefully placed it into a clear evidence bag and looked at both sides.

He bit his lip and shifted his eyes to Emily, then back to the note without moving his head. Then he ran his finger along the hairs of his three-day beard growth.

"I think you should see this," the detective offered and handed the piece of paper to the branch manager, who also read it silently and then handed the bag to Emily.

Emily, I think your smile is worth a million dollars. Would you have dinner with me? Tim Drucker 555-4625. For the second time, her face went ashen.

Author's notes: *I thought this was a great piece of mistaken intentions. I brought it to a critique group and there were much active discussion about the teller making the assumption it was a robbery and most people couldn't follow the logic.*

It became clear to me that many people in the group (and my other groups) needed everything spelled out exactly, which isn't my writing style. I realized it wasn't a piece everyone would understand, but that it probably wasn't flawed either.

I fixed a few of the other details people brought up but it really became clearer that my work doesn't please everyone and that I need to be okay with that.

ERROTICA

No one expected to discover Carl in bed with his girlfriend. For me, it was more of a shock given that the bed they were in was MY bed.

The room was dark with just the glow from the crack of the bathroom door frame lighting Carl's form. I barely made out the sound of a running shower in the background. My eyes were still adjusting to the darkness when I made out a second form in my bed. I focused my eyes on Carl.

Carl pulled the top of the comforter up to just below his old, saggy man-nipples. Instead of hiding them, it actually highlighted them, making me sorry I had focused on Carl. "Well, this is unexpected…" he offered.

"…and uncomfortable," I completed his sentence. A moment of silence followed, the kind which generally reserved for silent prayer. Mine was that I be teleported away by alien beings from the future who would mind-wipe me and then dissect me to understand the physiology of humans and overtake our race. I waited but nothing happened. His partner broke the silence.

"So how was work today, dear?" My mom's voice

came from the second figure. Damn. If she had never spoken, I could have focused on the old man nipples and been *less* disturbed.

"WHY don't you do this at your place…or Carl's place?"

"It's rude to not answer a question, young man."

"It's ruder for a mother to use her son's bed for her own carnal lust."

She sighed deeply, to indicate her impatience and inform me that I was being unreasonably difficult. "That nosy Mrs. Goldblatt across the hall - you know, the one with all the cats - well, she has an annoying habit of knocking at the door at the most critical moments. She always wants to borrow crackers or she's looking for her husband…"

I held my hand up, palm opened and facing them, the universal sign of please stop before I puke. "I don't think I want to hear this."

"It ruins the mood. Carl needs quiet or he can't...."

"And I really don't need to hear about THAT!"

"He can't even have music. It ruins the rhythm. Which is usually quite…."

"And THAT adds another six months to my therapy," I informed her. Mom snorted. The room reeked of something I couldn't quite recognize at first. "Did you light incense?"

"No. Well, kind of…" mom hesitated and Carl pulled his feet under the bottom of the comforter like a turtle retracting into its shell..

"Pot? You're smoking pot in my bedroom? Where did you get it? Why would you?"

"We ran out of whiskey," she explained matter-of-factly. Averting my eyes to the floor, I saw the sideways whiskey bottle on the floor beside a large stain on my new carpet. Mom turned her gaze to Carl. "He's always been conservative Carl.

When he was just a boy, he would get all freaked out when his sister Emily would see his little wee wee."

"It's not little," I nearly yelled. Mom always knew the exact thing to say to get me riled up. I think all moms take a class on it during pregnancy. Talk about your genitals using diminutive words; wave from the upstairs window in her bra to you and your friends; have sex in your bed with a guy when you're at work. It's all in the manual.

"He gets this way every once in a while, Carl."

"I don't get any way."

"Carl, watch this. Fuck. Fuck. Fuck."

"Stop it, Mom, just stop it."

"See, HE can say it if HE eats pizza with cheese that's too hot or stubs his pinky toe. But I can't say it, even if we are doing it."

"ABOUT to do it," corrected Carl.

"Oh my God, stop!"

I noticed that Carl kept glancing in the direction of the bathroom. "I think I need to…"

"No. YOU can wait." I didn't want to see Carl in his altogether naked state walking to my bathroom. I turned and looked at Mom for the first time. "How did you even get in here?"

"The emergency key you leave with me. We felt this was an emergency, Carl had been away for a week at Boca. Mrs. Goldblatt was nearby. So…"

"This is NOT your love nest."

"Well, of course not, dear. This is your place. We are just *borrowing* it."

"II think you're done. You two really should leave."

"I really should visit the bathroom," Carl repeated. He had a look of desperation.

"You can wait until I leave the room. I don't want to see...anything," I lowered my gaze to the floor again.

"We can't leave YET," Carl kind of whined.

"Why the hell not?"

They looked at each other, then turned their heads back to me. "Carl just took the big V, dear. It should be kicking in about now. We just need a couple of hours, honey. Why don't you go food shopping. There's nothing in the fridge and I've got the munchies." She giggled.

"No, no, no. A son should never see his mother and her boyfriend in any bed, especially in his own bed. This is the worst day ever!"

"Worse than the day you peed on the school bus in third grade? Worse than when your father and I caught you in the bathroom…washing?"

"Enough."

"I really do think I should…" but even as Carl said it, the room lit up as the bathroom door swung open and highlighted in the doorway was a very wrinkled 80 year old Mr. Goldblatt in an electric blue thong, making it crystal clear why he was always voted President of the Resident's Association.

"Are you ready? Daddy wants to *spank his niece and nephew for being naughty.*"

I stared a second too long, the image burning into my retina. I averted my eyes to the ground again. "I need to…go." I walked quickly out of the room and toward the door. "And please burn the sheets!" I shouted over my shoulder before leaving the apartment.

I gotta find someone new to hold my emergency key.

Author's notes: *This is my obvious attempt to flip the conventional and make the child the conservative and the parent the liberal of the story.*

LASTING IMPRESSIONS

I used my body to push her back against the inside of my front door. I didn't actually have to make contact with her to do it; she just kept backing away as my chest came close. I imagined her pressed so hard against the door that her shoulders and round ass left impressions like they have on my mind.

I had imagined a lot of things involving her. I imagined her sitting on my lap, feeling her round cushiony bottom on my thighs, playing innocent to me while the rest of the room gave knowing glances. I imagined her bending over and looking back to see if I was staring at the way her rear filled out her jeans. stretching her arms in the air to catching me staring at her chest pressing against her blouse. And I imagined spanking her through her jeans for intentionally teasing and flirting with me in front of others.

But most of all, I imagined her like I had her right now, pinned against a door and kissing her hard. Hard enough to surprise her from the guy who never breaks character, no matter what she says, no matter what she does.

Like last week when she offered me lunch. She grabbed my hot dog in her right hand and shook it at me as she made some point I can't even remember. She looked at me, looked at her hand and gave me that smirk before mumbling "Got my hand on your weiner NOW, shy boy" in a way she knew I could pretend not to hear…except my eyes gave me away. She stared right into them and then laughed before dropping the hot dog back onto my plate.

So now at the door, as she was leaving, I had done the unthinkable. Her own eyes widened and her expression changed: Surprise? Fear? Trepidation? It didn't matter. I pressed forward, finally making physical contact with her body and kissed her. I reach my arm around her waist and pulled her against me and kissed her in the most aggressive style I could muster, for this girl who made my passion bubble invisibly and had for years. She was trapped between the door and me with no choice but to feel my newly discovered assertiveness.

Then, mid-kiss, I was suddenly very aware of everything I was doing. I pulled back and looked at her, unsure once again.

"You went and ruined it," she said and stared at me.

"I did? How? You are always flirting…" I was still an inch from her face.

"We had this wonderful relationship. I flirt. You don't react AND MAKE ME WONDER…Does he know I'm flirting? Is he capable of flirting back? Does he even have a penis? I mean, I am attractive, aren't I," which came out as more of a statement than a question.

I answered it anyway. A puzzled "Yes," was all I could manage as I backed away.

"Most guys flirt back, at the supermarket, at the car repair, even that little old Asian man at the dry cleaner."

"Mr. Wang?"

"Yeah, Mr. Wang." She laughed, then snorted, then laughed louder. My gut tightened. "Just not YOU. You were consistent. So you were safe and fun."

"And now I ruined it," and I took another step back. "I'm sorry." I didn't know what to think. I clearly don't understand women, or what they are thinking or why they do the things they do.

"Yes, you ruined it," she said and stepped into the space I had just vacated, locked her arms around my neck before I realized what she was doing and pulled me to her face. She locked her lips on mine and pushed herself against me, kissing me back as hard if not harder than I had kissed her, if it were even possible. I was lost in her, tasting her mouth and the feeling of her soft chest pressing against me. She pressed herself against the side of my leg. Was that to make contact or avoid contact? I couldn't know for sure.

Then she broke the hold and moved back slightly. My eyes could focus on her face as she asked, "So whatever should we do now?" And the corners of her mouth turned up just slightly….still teasing, even after I made the move I never thought I would. She turned around and that perfect ass teased me again. I hooked the belt loop of her jeans with my forefinger and stopped her retreat. She spun around and, before I could react, she wrapped her arms around me, pulled me to her face again and I was back on the roller coaster.

“You’re as good a kisser as I imagined,” she murmured and moved back on my lips. As she imagined? She imagined me? When? I’ve seen her through at least a dozen boyfriends. Heavily muscled jocks. Geek fantasy game players. Pretty boys. They were all attracted to her. She didn’t have just one type. It was her personality and intellect. She was bubbly, smart and fun. She adapted to whatever was thrown her way. And her laugh.it was her laugh I personally found most attractive. Full and accompanied by accidental snorts that made her laugh more. You wanted to envelop yourself in that laugh.

Mid-kiss, she pulled back a little. I moved forward and she pulled back a little more, all the while staring at me with the slightest smile possible. After we have moved four steps, it became clear: she was literally making me chase her. Was I being played or seduced? Would I care if I could figure it out? I think too much so I just moved forward and quickened my pace. Her back was against the door again.

“Now that you have me where you want me…” she began… “Where do we go?”

“The sofa?”

“No. Figuratively.”

“Where would you like to go?”

She holds my head with her hands and brushes her lips against my jaw, then moves upward. "My intentions are to ruin you for anyone else," she whispers in my ear, then runs her teeth along the edge and earlobe. Goose pimples develop along my arms and neck. My entire body is ultra-sensitive. I think I'm in heat.

"I think you already may have."

"You think wrong. You have no idea."

My heart thumps loudly in my chest, threatening to explode. She must be able to hear it but doesn't comment. I'm confused, dazed. I have no idea what to do next. I go instinctual and wrap my hands around her waist, and pull her into me, forcefully. She mews into my mouth. "Mmmmm." She kisses me, then pulls away. "This was fun, but I have to go," she informs me.

"Really? Are you kidding me?" I don't understand what is going on.

"Maybe not really, but this is a good break…for you. Think about this. All of this. Then call me. Soon. I'll try to be available." She walks out the door and leaves me dazed. What the hell just went on?

It takes a full three minutes before I can move. My hands are shaking as I pick up my cell phone and dial her number. It rings a couple of times before she picks up. "Hello? Who's this?" she asks, knowing the answer already.

"What was all that?"

"That was foreplay," she tells me. "It was an introduction. Perhaps an induction. Maybe it was seduction." She was playing with words and with me.

"Why did you leave?"

"You let me leave."

"You said that you wanted to leave."

"I also wanted to stay. Did you want me to stay?"

"Yes. Of course."

"Then why did you let me leave?"

My brain hurt. Half of me wanted to throw the phone across the room, against the wall. The other half of me wanted to press her back against the door again. I held onto the phone. "I'm not sure I understand all of this."

"That's pretty obvious." There was silence.

"Can I see you again?"

"When?"

"Soon," I responded.

"How soon?"

"YOU seem to have all the answers. Why don't you tell me."

"No one is going to just hand you the keys to what you want. You have to make a little effort."

"Okay..how about tomorrow." There was silence again. "Around lunch time," I added.

"Tomorrow, huh? You can wait until tomorrow? I must not have made that much of an impression."

I realize I'm being played but I'm trapped in the game. "Okay, what about today?"

"When?" she asked.

"How about ten minutes?" I tried not to let my sarcasm show.

"You think it's all right to keep a girl waiting on your doorstep for ten minutes. That's not very gallant."

I tried to process the words even as I placed my hand around the doorknob and turned it. I didn't take the phone from my ear.

I heard "Oh, it looks like my date is here. I have to go," before I fully opened the door. The sun lit her from behind, silhouetting her figure like a solar eclipse, blotting out all the details. I know why the primatives feared the eclipse.

"You really are a piece of work," I tried to regain my composure.

"And I think YOU need some work. But I know a mechanic who is really good on guys like you. Let's get started," and she pulled the door closed behind her.

Author's notes: *I call this one erotica without sex, if that is possible. The challenge I gave to myself is to write a story that was arousing without having any sex at all involved. Sensual and evocative but no sex.*

While none of this story actually happened, it is based on a true story, kind of. There was a woman who seemed to play with my thoughts and feelings. In retrospect, I still don't know if it was on purpose or by accident. Although it never progressed past her teasing me in real life, I did imagine what would happen if I got further ensnared in her machinations.

My favorite comment was from one member of my writers group who said he wanted to punch the girl. I didn't plan to make her evil or bad...just playful and in control. I guess her personality really depends somewhat on the reader.

DINNER FOR TWO

I am caught in slow motion hell.

Tonight, my sixth grade son proudly wants to show me what he has learned in his Cooking Science class. I'm not sure how cooking qualifies as a science…I think that the nomenclature is much more about marketing in the wake of "Common Core" than anything else. Although it does sound better than the Home Economics tag it had when I was in the sixth grade.

As he s-l-o-w-l-y pulls together the ingredients prepare a one-eye jack (bread and eggs), I am thinking about all the work I still need to finish before I go to sleep. I still have four emails to send, and a proposal to prepare while he is in his "reading time."

After tapping a few notes into my phone, I see him FINALLY gathering the cooking utensils. He's not destined to be a short order cook. I look at the clock on the stove. We could have been eating by now if I were making the dinner. I should have assigned him clean-up duties which he could work at his own methodical pace. I resist the urge to say anything and just smile.

He continually pokes the still uncooked egg in the pan as a test, so I suggest that he turn the stove heat up. "But this is what my teacher tells me to do," he counters. I pull out my phone and start to write one of the emails. At this rate, I am in for a long night.

Finally, the egg cooks and he flips it over, poking it with the same spatula he did when the egg was raw.

"Seth, you know that touching the raw egg and then the cooked food means that you just put raw egg on everything…" and he turns to look at me with his Dark Seth look. I sigh and stop talking. I pray to whatever patron saint is responsible for safe eating that we don't get salmonella. After a few seconds, he goes and washes the spatula with soap and hot water. Sometimes a dad does know what he is talking about.

Finally, fifteen minutes later, we have two well done one-eyed jacks on our plates and eat them. They are (thankfully) fully cooked and tasty.

"Do you like them, Dad?"

"Yes."

"Really? You'd tell me the truth, right?"

"Absolutely," and I smile. Of course I wouldn't tell him the truth. But in this case I don't have to lie. "These are really good."

"We could have them for dinner tomorrow night of you want. Do you want to be my helper cleaning up?"

"I would love to be your helper." I watch as he meticulously cleans each instrument used in the cooking, using half of the bottle soap at the sink. I make a mental note to buy the less expensive store brand the next time I go to the market. My job is drying, which goes fast and easy. So I shift back to my emails for a few moments.

I look up from my phone and just like the food disappeared from our plates, he has disappeared into the other room to play video games. Suddenly, I am acutely aware of how wrong I was about all of this. Seth and I eating the first meal he cooked went *too fast*. I want this moment to last forever.

I walk up behind him and run my fingers through his hair. "What?" he says to me without turning.

"I'm proud of you. You made us a great dinner. I just wanted you to know. Thank you." He nods and smiles without taking his attention from the screen. I pull my hand away, thinking I have just blown one of the most important nights of his life so far. He turns to face me.

"Want to watch me play this game? I'm really good at it."

I think about the pile of work waiting on my desk. "Sure, I would love to." I put the phone on silent and turn it face down on the table. Then I plop onto the couch next to him. Sometimes a father needs to learn from his child.

Author's notes: *Another story inspired by a real-life experience with my son, Seth. Again, much of this is exactly how it happened. I think that makes it even more special. Sometimes child is the father to man.*

BIG WORDS

I'm watching… well, I'm really eavesdropping from the next table over, my presence partially obscured by a big stupid potted plant in exactly the wrong place. I'm in my favorite restaurant and I don't remember ordering the meal that is in front of me. That's because I'm way too interested in their conversation to eat.

"He's got big words and he knows how to use them," Betty whispered to Marge over lunch. Her friend's eyes widened.

"How big?"

"Big. Seven, eight, ten letters long. And full, thick sentences. When he speaks, he makes me squirm." She licked her bright red glossy lips then bit the lower one, releasing it slowly.

Marge knew then that this guy was special. Betty was generally attracted to the bad boys. Hell, they had even shared a few of them…at separate times, of course.

"He's a real writer. Daytime, he writes business plans and white papers. Deep stuff. At night, he writes to me. Texts, emails, flash fiction and short stories. He's even put me in a few." She giggled.

"Do tell, honey." Marge wanted details, the kind she could play back in her mind later when she was home alone, laying in bed.

"They're very personal." She offered with a heavy emphasis on *very*. Betty moved closer to prevent others from accidentally overhearing the stories she was about to tell. "In one, I was a princess trapped in a kingdom that wasn't mine and married to a sadistic swordsman, Prince Runemthrough. I was locked in a tower with no escape save for solving the puzzles of an ugly goblin named Enigmapaul, who was actually a handsome prince under an enchantment. In another I was a barnyard chicken, clucking and being chased by a cock." She giggled even as she said the word.

"Ohhh, I wish I had that kind of guy. Pierre buys me all sorts of gifts including that new Tesla and all the jewelry. But I've never had a guy put me in his story." Marge was seriously jealous. "Would you mind if I borrowed him? Just for an evening or three. I promise to return him without much wear."

Betty used her manicured hands against the table edge and pushed herself away. "No, this isn't one of those bikers with the engines that rumble beneath you or the blue bloods or...Pierre," she added more as a tease than anything else. "He's special. He's a writer. I'm keeping him for myself."

Keeping him? She had never ever heard Betty say those

words. Betty liked variety. There was a glow in Betty's smile and damned if the light reflected in her eyes didn't dance.

"Where did you meet writer stud?"

"A writers group."

"But you don't write."

"I don't hike either but I went to a couple of groups where other people do that, and climbed a few mountains, if you know what I mean."

"Can I see a pic?"
"Ok." She pulled out her cell phone and swiped past the photos of her well sculpted personal trainer and speedo-wearing pool boy until it landed on a bookish looking guy with glasses and a receding hairline.

"He looks like he gives good word. He has a big forehead."

"He does. I think…he just may be the one."

She turned the phone back to herself and as I leaned to the side of the plant, I could see the phone screen from behind the plant. It was a picture of me.

A loud horn blared, blotting out their voices but neither woman seemed to notice. Suddenly, they disappeared from sight. I stretch my arm over to press the button that would stop the sounds coming from the speaker in the small black box beside my bed. The world is so unfair, I think, as I force my eyes open.

I pick up the pen and pad I keep by my bedside. But instead of writing down the dream I know I will soon forget, I start in a different direction. Once upon a time there was a beautiful chicken…

Author's notes: *Pity the poor writer, who never gets the girl in the end. Everything and everyone is sexier than a writer, it seems. Well, except in my fantasies and in this story.*

CRAZY LOVE

What a great headline, she thought.

To the handsome EMT in Starbucks on Sunday: Save Me.

She loved looking through other people's postings in the Craigs List personal ads and especially the Missed Connection listings, peering into strangers' lives. She clicked the message to read further.

You saw me struggling to balance my purse and pay for my double shot latte, smiled and covered the tab. You touched my hand and talked about paying it forward. Your eyes sparkled and you quoted Thoreau: "The language of friendship is not words but meanings." How could you possibly have known that he is my favorite writer? For the first time in my life, words failed me. In my head we sat, we talked, we laughed, and I gave you my phone number. In reality, I only nodded and watched you walk out the door. Could we try a repeat with a different outcome?

Ellen could picture the entire event in her head. She could imagine the EMT's wavy brown hair, smell the mix of coffees in the air and even taste the foam off her upper lip. But most of all, she could feel the excitement of her heart racing faster, the butterflies in her stomach and the euphoria of something special being reawakened inside. More than anything, she wished THAT had been HER experience.

Then, her mind raced forward to what would happen if the man actually saw the posting. How would he? Maybe he would be on Craigs List to create his own posting, seeking the author out because of the connection he had also felt. Maybe he had been in a rush that day, receiving the call for an emergency that would eventually save someone's life. Maybe he just wanted to say more, to make a deeper connection, but just didn't have the time that day. He might be looking for her, too.

And when they did finally connect, it would certainly be sparks. Sexual tension would fill the air. How could it not? The attraction would be palpable to everyone in the room. They would see how the two fit together, like pieces to a puzzle long thought lost and finally found.

Of course, there might be problems. In her fluster, perhaps the author didn't notice the ring he was wearing, marking him as taken. But the fact that he was even looking in the Missed Connections was clear evidence that his current commitment was less than stable. That he was open to something more, something better. Something right.

Their chance meeting might result in...but no, it

wouldn't be chance. It would be fate, for both of them. Changing their lives forever. They would fall hopelessly in love and live out the rest of their days together.

She read the entire ad again and then a third time. This was the most romantic thing she had ever read. She could only hope that the author and the handsome EMT would eventually meet again and that their love would blossom.

She sighed with a smile and clicked "Okay," which brought up a disclosure, one that only those *posting* a message ever see. It described the liability of the person posting such messages, disavowing any responsibility for damages and the like. She clicked okay to that as well without reading it, authorizing the system to publish her ad. Then she closed the lid of the laptop, switched off the small desktop lamp and threw the towel over her shoulder.

Smiling, she walked through the dark hall back to her bedroom. She heard the loud and uneven snores of her husband before she even walked through the doorway. The room was dim with a vertical line of light shining through the opening of the bathroom door. She reached into her gown and retrieved an object which reflected a bright spot on the wall. She lowered the shiny chrome iPod so that the light bouncing from it wouldn't wake him, traced the cord back to the ear buds and placed them carefully into her ears and chose her "killer love songs" playlist.

Then quietly, she bent over her husband, tenderly kissed him on the cheek, and covered him with the sheet he had kicked off during his sleep. She reached into the other gown pocket and in a single motion, raised her hand above her head and brought the kitchen carving knife down through the sheet and into his chest. He suddenly woke and struggled as she twisted the knife left to right, then right to left with all the weight her small body could push behind it. Even in the darkness, she could see the sheet darken as his life's blood flowed from his body.

Only after his struggling ceased and the next song started, she pulled the knife out and wrapped it in the towel. Humming to the music, she made her way back to the guest room, also dark, and fluffed her pillows. She turned to her side, cuddled against the body pillow.

Suddenly, she sat straight up in the bed, the enormity of what she had done sinking in. How would she explain the body?

She thought of slicing the body into small pieces and throwing them out with the garbage. Too messy and honestly, too much work. The ground was far too frozen to dig a hole and bury it. She thought some more.

Then she smiled and reached for the phone. Her fingers pressed the numbers 9-1-1 and she waited patiently for the voice to appear at the other end. "Help, help!" she half whispered, inflecting a non-existent fear into her voice. "There's someone…here. My husband has been stabbed! He's bleeding. Send an EMT and police." She rattled off her name and address and clicked the phone off.

She walked to the bathroom and looked in the mirror. She applied fresh makeup and brushed her hair. If she was lucky, maybe they would send her new boyfriend. If so, she wanted to look her best.

Author's notes: *Thank goodness none of this actually happened. But I had a writer friend from years ago who would write ads in various Craigs List sections just to see the reactions, I guess. I decided to take it one step further as I wrote this story*

I wanted to start out as romance and make it turn into horror. In my writers group, I have one friend in particular who writes horror, so I wanted to see whether I could achieve several things with the one piece, including writing a piece he might give a thumbs up.

Of note is the fact that in two writers group critiques, only that friend liked the ending I originally wrote. Everyone else complained that they didn't understand the crazy lady doing what she did. "She's crazy!" was my answer but in the end, I listened to them and changed the ending to the way they wanted the ending to read.

I LIKE BEING CHASED

A girl who tells you this, up front, is offering you a warning. It's not a small warning, like *objects in a rear view mirror are closer than they appear*. It's more like the alarm sounds of a nuclear power plant AFTER releasing radioactive waste into the air. You probably don't want to be any place near the area but it's too late for the warning to do you any good.

I'm standing outside her door with a large bouquet of lilies behind my back. During our five dates, I've learned a lot about her including her favorite musicians (Sting and Bono); her favorite artists (Matisse and Reniore) and of course her favorite flowers (not coincidentally, lilies) - all useful facts for dating a pretty girl.

Despite my being on time, she makes me wait several minutes until the door swings open.

"Hi Jimmy."

Hi Heather," is the extent of what I can manage. It's always her eyes that always grab me first. People are often attracted to blue eyes or green eyes. Her eyes are brown and deep and pull you right into them. I stare into them and am lost in thought.

"Are those for me or do you have another date after this one?" Her smile transmutes the words from sarcasm to actually being funny.

"No, I mean yes...I mean no, I don't have another date and yes, they're for you." Why does this one girl affect me like this? By the fifth date I am usually showing a date my special move generally referred to by girls as The Twister, which generally guarantees me several more dates and being the center of conversation with their girlfriends. I meet a lot of my new dates that way.

She places the flowers in the vase strategically near the door without inviting me in. She quickly walks outside and closes door behind her.

"So where are we going?" she asks. I like the fact that she asks where WE are going and not 'where are you taking me'." I pay attention to the details on a date. Little things like that show who someone is beneath the surface. I also like the fact that she lets me be the man. She's perfectly happy being surprised with where I take her. So many women want to take control from the very start. And while I don't mind that, it often shows someone who can't NOT take control of everything.

"Not into your bedroom, apparently," I mumble without realizing it. I look at her for a reaction but there is none. Good thing I mumble very quietly. "How about to Scana's for dinner?"

"Oh, yummy," she offers and locks her arm in mine. And we talk while we walk the half mile to the restaurant. One advantage of living downtown is that you don't always need a car. It's a cool evening and walking ensures that we talk. I learn more about her family, her ex-boyfriends and the time she thought she was pregnant. So apparently she has had sex at some point. Thank you, God.

Through dinner, we talk. We laugh. And all of my focus is on her. As we make our way back to her place, I think that maybe, finally, I'll finally see the inside of her apartment.

I think wrong. Outside her door, she stands there, like a sentry for her own honor. "I can't invite you in."

"No? I don't understand. Don't you want me to…?"

"Of course I want you to. That's why you can't." Then she offers me a piece of information that I didn't expect. "Jimmy.." and she pauses for a second to focus my attention, "I only make the really special ones wait."

For maybe the first time in my life I'm dumbfounded. "But why.... And why would...?" I can't even manage to speak my thoughts.

"Shhhh. Think about it. You'll call me, right? I'd hate to accept someone else's invitation because I thought you weren't going to call." I nod with what must be the stupidest, most puzzled expression ever to appear on a human face. She leans in pushing her chest against mine, and offers me the sweetest warmest kiss I've ever felt in my life. Then she lingers longer than she needs to before pulling away.

"Thanks for the flowers, sweetie," she says and as she softly closes her door, and she tells me again, "Remember, call me."

You know, Maybe I misheard what she said in the beginning. Maybe her warning was *I like being chaste*.

Author's notes: *From what I remember about dating, it is confusing. I remember there being something about me that made women less likely to sleep with me no matter what their reputation was. I don't understand it to this day. It must be the presence of something or maybe a lack of something.*

In any case, I have the double-pronunciation of the title line in mind when I started and worked my way through that. Some pieces end up being dialog heavy...but this one is more in the mind of the primary male character. I kept the dialog to a minimum on purpose, to evoke a specific feeling.

INCONVENIENCE

"This is a stickup," she whispered. "Put all of the money in here," and she dropped the bulging baby tote on the counter. Her thick plaid scarf around her head and wide sunglasses that covered most of her face were unnecessary for 9:30 pm and should have been a clear clue as to her intentions.

"A stick-up?" the teenager repeated loudly in a vain attempt to alert anyone else in the area. There was no one. He had been alone for twenty minutes playing Candy Crush on his phone when she had walked in.

"Shhh, you'll wake the baby." The gun showed just below the baby she was lightly rocking in her right arm.

"But," he started again at full volume and she shushed him again, this time waving the gun a bit for effect.

"I know how bad this looks. It looks like I'm a bad mom. I'm not. I'm a good mom," she continued in a soft voice. "We had a schedule. Sitter comes at 9, I go and do my business…and this…and I am back by 10:30, 11 at latest. But my sitter cancelled at the last second. She's unreliable. I have a schedule. What was I supposed to do?"

The clerk just nodded and glanced toward his phone which started to buzz. "Maybe I should get that. It could be my mom."

"Just let it ring. We'll only be a few minutes. Open the register." She shook the gun lightly. "Just because I have the baby doesn't mean I won't shoot you if I have to…it just means that I'll aim for the boy parts. You understand?"

"Yes….sure…" He shook visibly and fumbled with the register, thinking about what a bullet might do to him.

"Open it." Her whisper was more forceful.

"I'm trying. I'm nervous, This is my first robbery."

"Well, let's see a little more opening and a little less shaking. I've got other stops to make. The supermarket, gas station…"

"You're robbing them, too?"

"No," she said as if it were obvious. "I have to pick up food for a dinner party I'm having this weekend. I'm not an animal, I don't rob *every* place I go."

"So why rob me?" He was still fumbling with the register.

"Good god, let me do it," and she moved behind the counter. "Hold him," and she handed the teenager the baby. She watched him cradle the baby in his arm for several moments, then scanned a pack of gum to open the register and scooped its contents into the bag. "How much you get paid for working in this dump?"

"$7.25 an hour." She smiled at him in a way that suddenly made him feel pathetic. "And all the fountain soda and day-old donuts I want. Sometimes I sneak a hot dog, too. That's gotta be worth another six bucks, right?"

She smiled again but in a nicer way this time, holding out her hands for the baby. "You're pretty good with the kid, despite being nervous for your first robbery." she said.

"I have a sister. She's eight now. But mom had a job so I took care of her a lot."

"Ever thought of sitting? Mine is useless and I could use someone reliable."

He started in the direction of the gun and then back to her face. "What's it pay?"

"More than this dump. Start you at ten an hour. You can eat *anything* from the fridge. And if I go on an excursion like tonight, I give you a bonus and bring home some extra fine snacks."

He didn't say anything, staring lower on her.

"What?" She asked.

"Your boobs, they're leaking through your top. I've never seen that."

She stared down at herself. "Crap, that'll ruin this blouse. Now I can't make my other stops."

Her face turned desperate as she stared him in the eyes as she waved the gun again. “I’m a woman, I have needs.” He took a step back from her. She quickly ran into the aisles with her baby still in the teenager’s hands.

“Right now, I need diapers and tampons.” She dropped them onto the counter. He didn’t move. “They’re just tampons. Grow a pair, will you?” They both looked down at the items that clearly wouldn’t fit in the diaper tote. The desperation in her eyes turned to anger. “And condoms. Three packs.” “Damn if I am ever going let this happen again.” He grabbed them from the space behind him and dropped them on the counter.

She stared down at the counter and without lifting her head mumbled, “No… the ribbed ones.”

His faced turned red as he reached behind the counter to fill her request and turned back to face her. “Paper or plastic?”

“Plastic.” Her demeanor changed quickly as he stuffed the items in the bag and handed over the bags and finally her child. “I have to run. Think about the sitter job.” She scooped up her bag and started to turn.

“How do I get in contact with you?”

She stared him in the eye, then grabbed a pen off the counter. “Here’s an email address. If you tell your boss or police about me or it, I’ll claim you tried to hit on me and file assault charges. No one will believe YOU.” She was almost out the door when she turned to him again. “I need a reliable regular sitter for three nights a week. It's very unprofessional to show up late or cancel at the last second. I don't stand for that shit. …You let me know." And she was gone.

He stared down at the open, empty register. What would he tell the boss? The last two nights his register was short over $40 each time which he falsely blamed on the previous clerk. Tonight it's empty from actually being robbed. That sitter thing was sounding pretty good.

Author's notes: *Completed in a day and a half. The idea came from a discussion with my very first girlfriend from high school. She is funny and we came up with the basic concept by tossing concepts back and forth over the phone. After hanging up, I was driven to write the entire piece.*

Like many pieces, it just flowed with just a few edits after the fact to clean up some of the rougher edges.

SELF HELP

The familiar, comforting voice spoke in the background offering the same positive suggestions he had heard over and over again. "YOU are in control." "No one can make you feel bad about yourself if YOU insist on feeling GOOD." "Make it happen. BELIEVE in yourself."

The words stung particularly hard. Nobody knew what was REALLY going on behind the public persona. The social media postings, the interviews, the news coverage: to an outsider, he seemed like the perfect, most successful business man that ever existed. Ironically, he was a failure in nearly every area of his life.

His company was facing almost certain bankruptsy. Foreclosure on his home was just days away unless there were some sort of divine intervention. And his soon-to-be ex lied just enough for the judge to place a protective order around his son, ensuring that he paid child support without unsupervised visitation rights. Taxation without representation, as it were.

What could he really learn from this self-help tape with the familiar voice? Nothing. Presentations like these were created by people to make money from other people who needed to get motivation and validation from strangers. In the end, they represent more wishes than truths.

Still, today was a big day; maybe the biggest ever. His new publicist had arranged a few of the most significant members of the press to attend his announcement. His brand new suit and shirt fit perfectly, the tie was pure silk and almost as expensive as his shoes. Good thing, because the purchase had tapped out his last available balance on his credit card.

The room lights were dimmed in preparation of the event. In the darkness, he adjusted the knot around his neck without the aid of a mirror. Not that it was all that hard. He had a lifetime of practicing knots, from his days in the Boy Scouts to every day in corporate America. He could and often did it with his eyes closed. This was his last chance to make a big impression on the people that would see him at the press conference. He twisted the knot to the left, then to the right until it felt the way it should.

People could be heard on the other side of the door, just minutes before the scheduled 10 AM press conference, when the publicist would let them in to the rented hotel ballroom. "He's making some last minute preparations," he heard the publicist say from the other side of the door and then, finally, saw the door begin to open. She was worth every penny she was charging, although he wondered how she would feel when she discovered that there was no money left to pay her bill.

He kicked the chair out from underneath him and felt the quick movement downward just before the sudden tightening around his neck caused a small snap before it all went black.

*　*　*　*　*

Self-help guru kills self while listening to own recordings the headline read. The news went viral reaching 3 million people while his final blog cast was read by 100,000 new visitors. Still enough to push his tapes to number one on Amazon for ten days running. His mother would be so proud.

Author's notes: *One of my favorite pieces that I have written. My not-very-disguised thoughts on people who claim to be experts and leaders in their fields. As a marketer, I find that life is 10% fact and 90% smoke and mirrors. I don't think I need to say anything more about that.*

I like to leave a lot of clues that makes sense after you realize what happens in the story. I think this one does that well. My favorite reaction was one of the writers group members audibly gasping at the next to last paragraph. That's like a standing ovation for a writer.

SOUNDS OF THE SEASON

Christmas carols are one of the sounds that remind me of the holiday as I was growing up. Mom played them in the background as the smells of her candied yams and gingerbread cookies filled our home. *My home* was always the gathering place on Christmas Eve. On Christmas morning, Mom, Dad, my brothers and I would make the two hour trek to Maryland and Aunt Dee's, followed by the half hour drive to Uncle Joe's and return home late that night. The back of the car would be filled with bags of gifts for us, replacing those we had taken for others. But it was *our house* that everyone chose for Christmas Eve.

The year I was ten, sixteen loud relatives crowded around the seldom-used dining room table. That table had been my grandmother's and looked it. It took people on either end pushing and pulling as Dad would direct us with "now" and "stop" to coordinate the action until we finally pulled the table far enough apart to insert the leaves.

Although I didn't know it at the time, this would be the Christmas I remembered the most. During the next few years, family would move out of the area and stop traveling to my house, and an argument of some kind would eliminate one or two of the others. Saddest of all, this would be the last one my Pop-Pop would attend. But for this year, the family was together.

“So, who wants dark meat,” my father would ask. It was his standard joke as the primary meat on the table was pork, ‘the other white meat.’

“I’ll have some,” my cousin Raelene spoke up while reaching for the potato dish. As she reached, her sleeve didn’t and exposed an elaborate tattoo with skulls, stitches and flames.

“A tattoo? I thought I forbid you from getting a tattoo,” Uncle Jake exploded. “Tattoos are for tramps.”

“You can’t tell me what to do with my body. And *I’m* not the tramp of the family,” Raelene yelled back. She didn’t name anyone specifically but stared at cousin Jolene, who might have stood to object were it not for the fact that her pregnant belly made fast movements impossible.

Instead, her Dad, my Uncle Ted, shot up as he slammed his utensils against the table. “At least my boy isn’t celebrating the holiday ‘up-state’.” No matter how angry anyone in my family was, they used the phrase *‘upstate’* when they really meant *‘in the slammer for stealing cars’*. I rode a couple of times with Uncle Jeff in his snazzy Camaro, his very cool Jeep, and his blue Thunderbird. I didn’t realize until later why he drove a different car every time I saw him.

“Please sit down! And be careful with the china,” Mom pleaded. She was down two setting since Christmas the previous year when Uncle Robert attempted to show the table his waiter skills and tripped on the rug.

I surveyed the table to see who had not yet entered the discussions. My brothers and I were too young to have done anything so wrong that would involve us. Pop-Pop was just returning to his chair; I hadn't seen him leave but he always seemed to be going to the bathroom. What a great time to return, I thought.

The commotion was loud in the tiny room, with shouting and fist banging blotting out the background carols. I lost track of who was defending who.

Suddenly, we all heard the loudest, wettest, most ripping fart any of us had ever heard. We all looked at each other trying to determine the source. After a few seconds of silence, my Pop-Pop spoke up.

"I'm sorry. Too much prune juice today, I guess. We all may want to move out of here for a bit."

Everyone quickly forgot the angry looks and words in their effort to leave the room as quickly as possible. The closest safe location was the den, so we all settled there, next to the tree. Parents in the chairs and sofa, kids on the floor; there was silence.

"Let's open some gifts." Mom reached under the tree and grabbed a box. "Sid," she announced and the box was passed from person to person until it reached the named family member. Each recipient read the label and announce who it was from, with the process being repeated until all of the gifts were distributed.

My family spent the rest of the evening thanking and kissing each other, and even singing along with the carols that played in the background. I don't remember if we ever went back to our meal. In the midst of those gift openings, Pop-Pop whispered in my ear, "Come out to the deck." I dutifully followed him out the back door and into the cold air.

"I'm an old man," he stared me in the eyes.

I smiled. "Not old."

"Old enough to know when things start to go off track and how to reroute them." I must have had a puzzled look on my face because he added, "One day that will make more sense to you."

Then he handed me an already opened box. "This is a gift for you. But given the commotion, I needed to borrow it." He patted me on the head. "I'm not sure whether I want you to remember this particular Christmas or not. But if you do, I hope that you will remember it in the right context. They may be a crazy family, but they're *your* crazy family. I love you."

Years later, even after I lost the remote control and the gift stopped working, I kept it on a shelf in the back of my closet. When I moved out of my parent's house, it made its permanent home in my memory box.

That battery-operated fart machine was a huge step up from the whoopee cushions I had previously owned, and for a ten year old, the best gift a kid could get. Especially because it restored a part of the Christmas magic.

Author's notes: *File this one as another "Can I take a distasteful topic and make an almost charming story about it?" That's always a very fun challenge, especially for me. Most people understood the story, but a few found it distasteful. Ah well...*

Most of this is fictional but like many of my stories, there are a few factual elements buried in it. The fart machine showed up in my family much later, when I stuck it in the carrier of my newborn son and used the remote to try to embarrass family members about his gaseous nature. Sadly, they all suspected something was amiss, presumably from knowing me so well.

My Pop-Pop was indeed the wise grandfather that this one is modeled after.

TODAY

Today was the first day he wouldn't kiss me goodbye.

It was cold and we waited in the car for the school bus' arrival. I asked him questions about what he dreamed about last night, which he answered curtly between bites of toaster-heated waffles. He's wearing his neon orange Under Armour sweat shirt for the third day in a row, despite my demands and pleas that he wear something, anything, that doesn't smell like stale wash. A six year old boy begins his journey to manhood early, I found, starting with the trading of actual conversations for the blasting of electronic villains on my iPad.

"So what happened when the truck in your dream started to fly," I asked.

"It just flew,"

"What kind of truck was it?"

"Green."

"That's interesting. You know, they say that many people don't dream in color. Do you?"

There is a long pause accompanied by the sound of an electronic ray gun and resulting explosions. "I said, most people don't dream in color."

"Oh. Cool." More electronic sounds.

"So what did you do in science yesterday?" I changed direction with a new and hopefully more interesting topic.

"Science stuff." Clearly I failed. I remember when he would tell me the details of his day, including bathroom stops and loud classroom farts from his best friend Joey. Was that just last week or ten weeks back? I have trouble differentiating between the two. Staring forward, trying to think of a different topic to engage him, I realize that I am out of time. The big yellow blob of a school bus stops 20 feet in front of the car.

"Bus!" I announced. He pressed on the pad a few more times with his grubby fingers before grabbing the overstuffed backpack lying on the seat beside him. His juice box, previously perched on top of it, falls to the foot area and begins a puddle I will need to clean up later.

"How about I hug you here" he stated and pushed through the opening between the front seats. The day was here, the one I most dreaded of all as the parent of a young boy. He gave me a big hug and my eyes watered, grateful for what I was being given and saddened by what I was not. I was lost in my thoughts until I looked up to see him climbing the step into the bus and disappearing from sight. No wave, no looking back.

The bus gates closed, the vehicle expelled an ironically appropriate gassy sound and it was off, taking my son to another day of events I would never really be told about.

I thought about how fast things change despite my efforts to keep them the same. My vision got blurry and I wiped my eyes with my sleeve, then I shifted the gear stick into drive and began my work day.

At least I still get the hug.

Author's notes: *While not the exact conversation we had, it's not too far off. Fatherhood is such an awesome experience, but sad in many ways also. Definitely in line with my feelings of that day.*

WORKING STIFF

I am watching him through my side and rearview mirrors. He weaves dangerously through the traffic, his bright red 2014 Camaro hugging too close to the bumpers of those in front of him as he seeks an opening to move left and right. No turn signal, no warnings for the people around him. He gives them no choice but to step on their brakes to give his car the room it demands.

That fool is going to die today is all I can think as I watch the car quickly and without warning swerve into the adjacent lane once again. He ends up two cars directly in front of me.

Traffic slows to 25 miles an hour and even without seeing his face, I feel his impatience. As soon as we pass the construction sign, he swerves onto the shoulder and accelerates to his former speed, passing his slow-moving obstacles.

I am in no rush myself. Long ago I realize that nothing really important happens until I get where I am going. That's one of the advantages of working solo. Given that conclusion and the fact that I never really worry about money, I can honestly say that I enjoy my work better than I did before the revelation. Instead of racing like that guy, I have the ability to see the bigger picture in all things I do.

I drive a deep purple 1982 hearse for the novelty of it. I had red and orange flames placed on the hood and sides as a joke and maybe to attract a little attention. The truth is, no one ever seems to notice me. They're generally distracted by expensive stretch Hummers, concept cars and high end German imports that are a mainstay of the roads in L.A.. As colorful and unusual as my car is, it hardly attracts any attention. But that's okay...I like it and it is highly functional.

The slowed traffic started moving again. I approach a stretch of highway-damaged metal guard rail, arbitrarily colored with swashes of paint scraped from the cars that have sideswiped them. They tell the stories of drivers distracted by texting, phone conversations or arguing children in their back seats. But seen another way, the side rails are more than a functional structure. They are works of art, formed and deformed by unplanned moments and movements. They could never be exactly duplicated much like two snowflakes could never duplicate one another. Each is unique and beautiful in its own way.

It's just a few minutes later that I found my speedy friend's car stopped on the shoulder, the result of colliding into a construction vehicle. His car looks as though the front end has exploded, spewing debris all around. The car has shed its outside panels like a snake's skin, exposing a crumpled metal frame. Bits of windshield safety glass reflected sunlight like a grade school glitter project but telling a more ominous story.

I pull my car just ahead of Mr. Speedy's and over onto the same shoulder. I couldn't believe that anyone could survive a wreck like this, but I needed to be sure.

There hasn't been time for police or fire or emergency care to respond, but a few good Samaritans are there. One is bent at the waist, throwing up in the grass to the side. Another has his cell phone to one ear and his hand blocking the other, facing away from the accident. Traffic continues past the scene, with occupants gawking through the windows and shaking their heads.

The driver, the man who I assume was the driver given the deep cuts on his face and blood smeared clothing, stands alone looking dazed. I extend a hand. "Let me help you." He's visibly shaken but puts his bloody hand in mine. I walked him over to my car. He looks at it, puzzled by the make and color scheme, but then give a small smile.

I hold the car passenger door open as he carefully lowered himself into the seat. "Don't worry about the blood. I can get the seat cleaned later. And don't forget your seat belt," I grin at my little joke; he grins back and attaches the buckle. I put on my turn signal and merge easily into the traffic.

"Good thing you happened along," are his first words to me. "I know I was driving wild but I was trying to get to my daughter's school recital. She's seven and lives with her mother. I don't get to see her that often."

I smile. "I can take you where you need to go…" As I say the words, the truck directly ahead of us suddenly changes lanes and the bright light previously blocked suddenly hits the windshield directly, blinding us both momentarily. I speed up and fill the truck's spot on the road. "…but we'll need to make a stop," I complete my sentence.

He puts down the sun visor to cut the glare. "How far do we have to go?" he asked.

"Not far. Just into that light up ahead."

Author's notes: *Another story designed to take the reader in one direction while dropping hints about the true nature of the characters. It's fun when I actually can pull it off and learn where people have their "aha" moment.*

YOUR PAST SNEAKS UP BEHIND YOU

I'm standing at the urinal, concentrating on the speech I need to give. But even if I wasn't, I have a rule: I don't like guys talking to me when I'm standing in the bathroom with my friend in my hand. That rule is doubly applicable when the other person is a woman, standing behind me.

Focused on my task at hand, I hadn't heard her enter. "So, how are you doing there?" She asks me.

"I'm a little busy now," I offered curtly. "And distracted."

"I can see that."

"Do you have a reason for being here?" I asked while moving closer to the urinal to block a view she doesn't have anyway.

"Seeing what you guys have in here."

"Mostly urinals, toilets…and men." I emphasized the last word. "This really isn't helping me pee,"

"I suppose not." She paused. "You're Tim, tonight's speaker, right? You don't recognize me, do you?"

"Not by voice," I answered, staring at the wall. "Should I?"

"I guess not. It's been a long time. I'm Holly Newman."

The name seemed vaguely familiar but I didn't know from where. "Hello, Holly-in-the-men's-room. Is there something I can help you with?"

"You won't remember me, but I remember you. Second grade. Brandywood Elementary. Mrs. Thompson's home room."

I remembered all of it except Holly Newman. "If you want to schedule a class reunion, I can give you my email address. I'm kind of occupied here."

"You saved my life. I was walking home from school. There were three older guys. They came running up and knocked the books from my hands. They started teasing me about being a Braniac. I was chubby back then. They called me piggy-wiggy black blotch because I'd gotten my pants dirty that day. I stood there as long as I could before I sat down and started to cry. Suddenly you were standing in front of me and said, "Smart girls shouldn't have to put up with crap from stupid guys." They left. You picked up my books and told me to ignore them. You were my hero."

It sounded so familiar and then, suddenly, the moment snaps into my head. But I remember it differently than she described. I'm nine, walking from school with my friends. I pointed out Holly and her pants that look like she pooped them. I laughed, the guys laughed and they decided to teach the class Braniac a lesson. I watched in horror as they physically bullied her. Rescuing her from something I started hardly made me a hero or even an innocent bystander.

I did a lot of insensitive things when I was younger. I embarrassed people. I took their feelings for granted. I hurt them to make myself look or feel bigger. There's nothing as uncomfortable as hearing a story about your younger self and knowing you stood on the wrong side of the stupid line.

I open my mouth to tell her the truth and apologize but nothing comes out. Nothing. My mind just replays the scene over and over and I stand there. Finally, my mind goes back to her voice thanking me for being her hero.

"No need to say anything…or turn around," she laughed. "I just wanted to say thank you."

Silence. Finally, I find some words, still facing the wall. "I need to tell you something," I start and wait for a reply. There is none. For the first time, I turn my head and in my peripheral view, I see…nothing. I turn my head the other way and see only another guy at the other end of the far counter. "Did you see the lady who was just here?"

"A woman? In the men's room? They sure have balls these days," he chuckled. "Nope, but I just walked in here myself so I might have missed her."

"But she was just…" my voice trailed off.

I finally managed to pee, tucked myself in and went to wash my hands. As I looked into the mirror, I saw a middle-aged man with grey on the temples…and past behaviors that embarrass him to this day. The soap dispenser drizzled soap onto my hands and I spent too long mindlessly rubbing them together under the hot water stream. I looked down blankly before shaking them off and reaching for the paper towel.

I took out my typed notes for the after-dinner speech I was scheduled to deliver. They always expect the honored guest to say something. I look it over and unconsciously shook my head. How did I even think that I could deliver this?

I placed the papers down on the sink and pulled out a pen. Suddenly, I was inspired to make some changes. So I did. Then I stuffed the papers into the inside pocket of my suit coat and walked back to the head table.

"Are you okay, you look flushed?" My wife asked. She puts her hand on my leg, squeezes and leans forward to whisper in my ear. "I know you hate these things, but this isn't really about you. We're raising money for a good cause. And you have done some great things for the community. Relax. It's okay to be in the spotlight for a few minutes."

They called my name and I walked to the podium. I scanned the audience for Holly Newman, but I didn't expect to actually find her in the crowd. It doesn't matter. I knew she was there. I could feel her.

"It's an incredible honor to be here tonight surrounded by family, friends, and people who have been roped into buying tickets," I start. I get my first laugh. And I begin to tell a story I'd long forgotten.

Author's notes: *I am sadly aware of some of my failings in behavior growing up...and even now. There's no real way to make all the apologies we should. Wouldn't it be nice if we could? Sometimes the only route is to fix and be aware in the present and guide those around us toward making better choices than we did back then.*

FIRST KISS

We're talking, faces close. Hers just inches from mine, with lips so near I can almost taste them. The vanilla scent of her hair washes over me and churns my stomach in knots, making it hard to think straight. I am 16 again, despite being well, well past that. I crave her in a way that almost hurts: she makes me feel empty and full at the same time. Watching her lips move, seeing her smile at her own comments, the world moves in slow motion. She radiates from the inside out, although her outside is strikingly beautiful, too.

Look at someone up close, as close as I am to her, and people appear different. Maybe it's the change of focus or reference points that disappear with the changed field of vision. Lines and dimples become their own elements instead of negative space between other features. Staring into her eyes, I see sparkles of light reflected from around the room. My breathing is erratic and my heart is thumping loudly in my chest. It's all I can hear and interferes with my hearing her voice.

"Shhhhhhh," I interrupt her speaking mid-sentence. Her words cease and lips close against each other. I quickly press my lips on hers, holding her gaze. It's a test to see how our lips fit together…they do, like matching parts of a puzzle. My hands unconsciously grip her hips to pull her closer. Lip contact becomes body contact. It's not so much sexual as it is animal, instinctive. I want to pull her straight into my body and for that moment merge with her completely. My hand slides from her hip to her back, pulling her closer; my tongue lightly touches her lips, then runs a gentle line across the edge of her perfect teeth. The animal takes over and I lightly bite her lip, feeling the puffy flesh slowly slide from the grasp of my front teeth. One of us moans ever so slightly, I'm just not sure who.

I pull away slowly, s-l-o-w-l-y still holding her stare, still holding her back. I want my hands all over her, to rub her whole body against mine and mark every part of me with her scent so that others know. The sounds of my breath are ragged and heavy, as though I have just finished a race, when in truth my race has just begun. My eyes refocus at the new distance and project all of my thoughts, the stories from my head that involve me and her together that haven't yet happened. I watch as she bites her own lip and I am lost, so completely lost in this moment. And in her.

She smiles again and the rest of the room comes back into focus. The table we are standing next to, the chairs to our side, the waitress trying to step around us but blocked from her destination. The crowds of people milling around and the others staring at her and I, staring at each other.

Best first kiss ever.

Author's notes: *I wanted to write something romantic, that conveyed the magic and butterflies of a first kiss. I reached into my memories to combine the feeling I had with a number of first kisses, so while this isn't actually one first kiss, you could call it several of them.*

All the more special when you compare and realize that most first kisses are not like this one.

WHERE DO I COME FROM?

That is the question most parents nervously anticipate. Our anxiety surrounds the question of *how much* we tell, *what depth* we reveal…and how much our little urchins have already discovered through discussions on the school bus, from after-care and from their own and their friends' siblings.

However, for adoptive parents, there are more pressing worries. Our concerns go to a very different place. How much will my son want to know about his birth parents? Will my daughter feel that she was originally "thrown away" and will it affect her self-esteem?

"Daddy, where did I come from?" my five year old son Seth asks again, and I realize that I am going to need to answer him one way or another. I take the easy route.

"Well," I start, "when a Mommy and a Daddy are in love, they decide to share that love. So they do something special." I pause on purpose, to see whether it's enough. It isn't.

"Is it something they eat?"

I want to badly to make a comment here but I resist. "No." is my only answer.

"Well, what is it?"

I pause again. "We don't talk about it. They just do it. And then a baby starts to grow in the Mommy's tummy."

"No," he changes direction. "I mean my birth Mommy. Was she pretty?" And the conversation takes a turn much worse than explaining penises and vaginas, and the interaction between the two.

"Yes," I answer. "She was pretty." I opt to answer only exactly what he asks, kind of the approach a lawyer would give you if you were facing a criminal trial.

"And was my Daddy tall?"

"Birth Daddy," I correct him, wincing just a little. "Yes, he was tall."

"So I might be a basketball player when I grow up?"

"Could be. It depends on what you want to be."

He goes silent and I feel like I may have dodged a bullet. Until… "Why did they give me to you?"

His question is a sharp reminder that there is a part of our relationship I can't control. There will be many in the future, but this one will always be the scariest to me. So I refer back to a story I've told him nearly since the time he could talk. It's part of my attempt to inoculate him. But he's grown up and at the age where he uses logic now. I hope that the story still works.

"Well, you know the story of Superman, right?"

"Yes. His planet was going to explode so his Mommy and Daddy put him on a rocket and sent him to Earth to be safe."

"Right. Well your birth Mommy and Daddy (emphasizing the word birth) loved you but weren't ready for a baby, But they wanted you to have a great home. So they made a sacrifice to keep you safe and happy."

"Oh," he nods as if he is thinking about the story for the first time. I use the slight pause to prepare myself for the next question, the ones that are a logical extension. Maybe 'Do I have a birth brother or sister (he does) and why did they give me up but not them?' There's no good answer to the question except my dumb luck. Those are questions I will have to answer one day. But as it turns out, thankfully not today.

"And Captain America's shield? How come it never gets dented when it get shot with bullets?" Finally questions I am more comfortable answering.

"Because it's made of a special metal, Admantium. Why don't we go to the toy store and see if they have any Cap action figures?

Today ended happy for both of us. It may not always work out that way when he asks questions. But we've both happy as we climb in the car to create another important father-son memory.

Author's notes: *This is actually not far off from the actual conversation my son Seth and I had, and the ending is accurate. Sometimes life imitates art.*

THREE WORDS

To be the first to say the words out loud is risky. No matter how long it's been, it still may be too early. There is probably some unwritten rule on how long you wait before you actually speak them so that you don't seem like a crazy person or off balance or worse yet, needy or insecure. But I don't know the rule.

She stands before me, a goddess of curves. At 21, she's two years older than I am with three serious relationships before ours. She's more worldly and experienced than I am. I stand on the train platform, flowers in hand, two bunches of roses pressed together because one just didn't seem big enough for how I feel.

My heart is bursting and I want to say the words that repeat inside my head. But if I do, they will make me seem emotionally weak when what we have is really a friendlier version of friends with benefits. Maybe they'll mark me as a child, highlighting my inexperience in relationships. Maybe she has been trying to evaluate what she feels and my declaration will be the final straw to push her away. Or…

And then, my time is up. She is on the platform in front of me. Did she walk casually or run on first seeing me? Her tight jeans highlight her slender legs and curves of her rear. Her face is flawlessly smooth, her hair long and free, blowing in the breeze. Her bright red lipstick competes for the attention the sparkle in her blue-green eyes demand. Lost in thought, I missed my opportunity for a clue to guide my decision. She kisses me full on the lips while her hand finds the back of my head.

“Mmmmm” helps me delay the moment.

She pulls back. “Is that all you have to say?” Her eyes narrow just a bit and her words dare me, hinting at something even if I don’t know exactly what.

“I missed you.”

“That’s better,” but I can’t tell if the time between my comment and hers is a pause or not. She takes the flowers from my hand and pulls them to her face. She inhales. “Beautiful.”

“Yes you are.”

“What?” She looks up and I’m not certain whether she’s playing with me or really didn’t hear my words.

“I could fall in love with you so easily.” The words are out before I realize I’ve said them. But they are a compromise, a safety net. Intentions but a lack of commitment. We both know it. She looks at me, then down at the flowers. Without seeing her lips move, I hear it, barely. “I know.”

There’s silence as we walk hand in hand to the car. I’m confused. Is she happy? Insulted? Scared? Do women just have different rules? What the hell are they? The sounds of the car radio thankfully drown out my thoughts.

I spend most of the weekend trying to forget that moment and living in the next one. We race around, having no real life constraints. An afternoon picnic in the park, an evening concert that night, an early brunch at a fancy restaurant the next morning.

And at the end of the weekend, we are back at the train station and parting with a kiss. A book end to the one that started the weekend, but without the flowers. Passionate, hands behind my head again. The butterflies take over as the train pulls away and I start making mental arrangements for the weekend I will go see her.

A couple of days later on the phone, we get into a fight over something so insignificant that I can't even remember what it was. We break up, long distance. I'm heartbroken and worse still, I have no idea of her thoughts about it. I often wonder whether she knew ahead of time that was to be our last weekend together.

* * * *

And here I am, now, 30 years later. The train station is replaced by a restaurant lunch but the two bunches of roses are the same, at maybe three times the cost. I stand in the entrance, waiting for her. Women passing by may be guessing this is a first date but it isn't...it's easily been three months since I began seeing her and I still get butterflies. She consumes my thoughts and makes me crazy. And I haven't yet said it.

I've come close. But the timing was wrong, or it was too public, or something happened as I was about to, or…

And once again, I miss the actual entrance and already she's in front of me. This woman is different than that one from my past. Her dress is conservative as is her lipstick. She wears the wrinkles of experience; glasses and pulled-back hair give her that smart librarian look. I find her stunning. She smiles at me and I hand her the flowers. "These are for you."

"Of course they are. You always bring me flowers. You're incredible," and she reaches up to kiss my cheek. Her free hand reaches out for mine and squeezes it, the middle-aged equivalent of public passion with less embarrassment. Inexplicably, the feeling I get is as overwhelming as I remember the kiss at that station so long ago.

The intervening years have taught me the complication about relationships. Expectations both met and unmet, give and take, the illusion of control, the significance of timing…everything it seems except the confidence in saying the words.

She brings the flowers to her face to smell their scent. My stomach twists for the present and the past.

"I love you, you know." This time, my words are a conscious choice.

"Of course I know. It's about time you said it…out loud," she scolds me. "I've been in love with you since the day we met."

"Then why…?"

"Because I want the man who is willing to take risks. I need the man whose passion drives him to act. The man who I inspire to take risks."

I wrap my hand around her waist and pull her into me. I kiss her hard. Her hands move to the back of my head. Not what is expected from middle aged people in front of the restaurant reception desk. My heart beats faster and my mind is racing. I realize we are in the wrong place at the right time. "Let's skip the restaurant and go for a picnic in the park. A fast stop at the market and we'll have everything we need." I don't wait for an answer and pull her out the front door.

She breaks into a wide smile. "That sounds perfect."

Author's notes: *The beginning involving a transportation platform is pretty true to the hazy memory that I have of the time, as is the challenge of being the first to say the words. And the line "I could fall in love with you so easily" was one I actually spoke to a different girlfriend to test the waters for a reaction. Making yourself vulnerable is complicated and risky.*

When writing this, I didn't expect that readers would think that the first girl was the same woman later on, but some did. I do like leaving some obliqueness in my writing so I was pleasantly surprised by that assumption. Whether it is or isn't is up to the reader.

NEGOTIATIONS

She pulled her blouse open to expose her breasts to the stranger in the back room. “Well, how about this?” she asked, clearly confident that she already knew the answer.

“Are they real?” he asked. The question used to make her angry but she had learned to just smile in response. Of course they were real. Who in their right mind would do this to themselves on purpose?

Men spent so much time focused on them, stealing glances and even copping a feel as though they were objects and not an actual part of her body. For the 20 years that followed puberty, her one constant goal was to make people appreciate her value without it being directly related to the size of her chest. That wasn’t easy. Boys from school had entire conversations staring at them. She’d catch work associates pretending not to do the same thing. Even her bosses had trouble looking her in the eyes.

She’d gone through extraordinary efforts to hide them, using thick sweaters and shapeless tops, and at one point even (painfully) strapping them down; everything short of having actual reduction surgery. All her efforts succeeded in doing were to make her look frumpy and unattractive. She cried even as her girlfriends revealed how they secretly wished that theirs were more like hers and that they were the recipients of all the attention she received from the boys.

But in her thirties, she became more comfortable with herself, her talents and *the girls*. She would never give them actual names, like guys do with their dicks. That seemed weird and schizophrenic, as if the genitals lived a life of their own. Well, maybe for guys they do…but *the girls* seemed less offensive and less medical-sounding than breasts. Chest seemed like the right word for guys, not girls. And why the hell would anyone call them boobs? Unless it was for the effect it had on guys who looked at them.

With the comfort came confidence, more attractive clothing and just a bit of cleavage showing. Then, more. Instead of feeling embarrassment, she discovered the empowerment they gave her in situations.

"Not bad," the greasy man squinted and cracked a smile.

"Not bad? Really…maybe I should just put them away," and she reached to close her blouse.

"No, Good. Really good." And he continued to stare at them.

She slowly released a practiced, innocent smile revealing her perfectly straight and very white teeth. He didn't see them or the money her parents had spent on their straightening. She pulled her blouse open again and, this time, shook them a little for effect. The man had a stupid smile plastered on his face. His parents should have spent a few bucks on *his* teeth, she thought. She continued to smile anyway.

"So we should talk about price," she began.

"$400."

"$400? Really? I don't know why I even came back here with you. I think you can do better."

"Okay…$375," he countered.

She started to re-button her top. "I know you can do better. I don't think you really appreciate this."

"Oh I do, I really do, but there IS a limit."

"Well, think about that limit better and we'll speak again…some other time. Well, unless I find another taker across the street," and she closed the top.

"Wait, I could do $300."

"That's more in the neighborhood," she smiled. "Which reminds me, you know where to show up?"

"Yeah, I have your card."

"Good. Thursday. 3 pm. I'll be there waiting."

"Normally I need a two-hour range…"

She laughed at his unintentional play on words. "Sorry. I have a busy day, you know. Be there at 3. I'll be waiting for you, honey." She blew him a kiss, secured the last blouse button as she left the back room, and walked across the crowded floor to the expectant stares of men trying to hide their preoccupation from their wives. She crossed the parking lot to her waiting car. The passenger door was unlocked and she slid into the seat.

"So, you finished up in there?" the man in the driver's seat asked.

"Yep."

"How much?"

"$300."

"Goddamn. That was $100 lower than the price I negotiated with them yesterday."

"What can I say. Big Tit Discount. You aren't built for that. The oven is being delivered on Thursday. Something tells me that store owner may make the delivery himself. You may want to hang around and watch his disappointment when he sees you there, too," she giggled.

"I love you."

"Look me in the eyes when you say that, buster."

Author's notes: *My first written piece once founding the writers group and rediscovering my writers "voice." This was an intentional attempt to capture in words a perspective men can't really understand. The "big tit discount" phrase came from a past girlfriend who used her magnificent chest to her benefit on many occasions. I always found that funny...and clever.*

What I enjoyed most about this piece was the confusion I cause with the price going down instead of up, causing the reader to wonder what is going on before the final "reveal." Done on purpose to disorient the reader and hopefully, the final pay-off makes up for it.

Originally published online at smashedcat.com.

MISDIRECTION

It's the same argument every time the two of them are in the car together with me.

"Don't listen to her, she's telling you the long way. Turn left here and then go straight," my wife commands. I don't offer any thoughts out loud because I know that tone of voice all too well. I fiddle with the dashboard sound controls to get the entire music balance going to the back speakers. She gets annoyed when she has to compete with the radio.

"Make a U-turn at the next intersection," the other woman's voice, refusing to acknowledge my wife's comments or presence. I grip the steering wheel tightly enough that I see my knuckles turn white when I should be watching the road.

"Don't listen to her," my wife instructs again, not looking back. This is a mistake, I know it. But it's too late. Is there a part of me that subconsciously believes that I deserve it? That could explain being in this position.

"You know I'm right," my wife intones. And with those four words, I know what's coming. All of it. Proof positive of her rightness. "I was right about the roof leak and that we should have fixed it before the fall." She doesn't mention the sheet rock sagging and then falling on her grandmother's teapot collection; the stare she gives me is enough. "And the washer, the tree in the back yard that nearly destroyed the living room, the finger paints that you gave the kids..." All couples use shorthand phrases that represent entire stories mostly so they can fit more examples into a single breath for maximum impact.

Then it gets really personal. "I was right about your mom's boyfriend, and that woman from work who was flirting with you, and…."

Of course, there's stuff she's been wrong about, as well. She was wrong that my sister would like the painting we bought for her birthday. You would think that the fact it isn't hanging anywhere in my sister's house might be a clue. It apparently isn't. And she was wrong about which direction to store all the records I'd had since being a teenager. They are all incredibly warped and unplayable, just as vinyl has made a comeback. And she was wrong about how long you can drive a car before you change the oil. Boy, was she wrong about that. There's more, but as I look over at her, I'm convinced that she can read my thoughts. I immediately switch to thinking about the music on my iPhone and other things that will get me in less trouble.

All this time, the other voice is wisely silent. When she finally does speak again, she stays annoyingly on topic. "Turn left on Ash Avenue." Couldn't she focus on anything else?

"Wrong. There's always traffic there. It's backed up this time of day. And the Christmas tree leaning too much…half my ornaments broke that year. I was right about that. And…"

I begin to hum lightly to myself, which the wife unfortunately hears.

"Are you tuning me out?"

"No, of course not," and I am telling the truth, kind of. I may be trying to tune her out but I since I'm not succeeding, my answer seems at least not a full-out lie. "You know, there's nothing wrong with a second opinion," I state without thinking.

"Make a left turn at Orange Street," comes the other voice right precisely at the wrong time.

"Orange? Who the fuck would turn on Orange? That's a neighborhood, for God's sake. And remember the time we went to Reading. Her directions rode us in circles…" I do remember that incident, although I think the two of them talking over each other was part of the problem. I don't offer that up.

"You're right," I nod. I entertain visions of purposefully driving into the guard rail and flipping the car down from the overpass onto another car and into a fiery wreck or, if I'm lucky, a full fuel tanker. The thought is calming.

The two continue their back and forth independent direction-giving until I finally can't take it anymore. "Please stop," I blurt out as I pull the car onto the shoulder of the road. There is a moment of silence nearly as scary as the previous din.

“This isn’t a big deal. We’re just going to the supermarket ten minutes away.” I ask my wife which direction to take.

“Just go straight four blocks, then turn left at the light.” I pull away from the curb and exactly two blocks later, run into stopped traffic. Blinking red and blue lights and a downed electrical cable. With cars quickly stacked behind us, there’s no space to turn around. Trapped.

For my own safety, I only look straight ahead. I turn up the music to fill the uncomfortable silence. And then I hear that little sweet voice say one last thing. “Heavy traffic ahead. Recalculating.”

Author’s notes: *Again, relationships can be complicated. Some of us just want to get from one place to another. Our priority may be speed...comfort...peace. Others have a specific route in life that figuratively or literally involves the word ‘right.’*

MISTLETOE

The mistletoe hung above me, daring me to take action. I had spent half the night standing beneath it, protecting my territory and trying to find an inconspicuous way to get her to join me, here. That isn't easy to do when the 'her' is the cutest girl in the room and a social butterfly.

Danielle was my fantasy girl, who was always dating a friend, a friend of a friend, or some other guy without friend as part of the descriptor. The one I could never have and who renders me incapable of speaking in full, coherent sentences. I first met her at a party like this one three years ago. I just hadn't found the right time to make my move.

Given the fact that she finally made her way over to me, now should probably be that time.

"So it's Christmas," I said.

"Yes it is." She smiled.

"And here we are, here I mean, together, again, well, not *together* together, but in the same place, at this party, together…"

"Yup, party. Here. " She turned her head left, then right, as though she were looking for somewhere else to be. Then she stared me in the eyes. Even disinterested, she was incredibly pretty. Mistletoe. Pretty girl. Christmas party. Me. Which of these things was desperately out of place?

Two guys, one her recent ex according to the scuttlebutt, made a straight line toward us on his way to the free beer. Scuttlebutt. Where did that word ever originate, I wonder, as I tried to come up with more single word sentences to utter.

"Hey Deanie," the ex slurred and grabbed a handful of her ass as he walked by. She giggled and then looked me in the eye. "I wish he would stop doing that. It's totally inappropriate and embarrassing." I nodded in agreement but the entire time wonder what her ass would feel like in *my* hand. Could she possibly see what I was thinking through that stare. It was a powerful stare.

She broke the awkward silence. "Hey, that's mistletoe, isn't it?" she asked, pointing up and interrupting my ass-in-hand thoughts.

I feigned ignorance and looked up. "Oh yeah, I guess it is." How lame, even for me.

When I looked back down, she was suddenly on tiptoe, an extra three and a half inches taller. Her hands shot up around my neck and pulled my head down. Her chest pressed into me as her lips pressed HARD against mine. This wasn't an "I'm under mistletoe and I'll kiss on the cheek because its tradition" kiss, but more like "I'm kissing you full on the lips with my beautiful soft mouth in a way you always hoped for" kind of kiss.

This was the moment that I'd replay every time I see her with the then-current guy she'd be dating and wish it was me.

The kiss knocked me off balance…literally. Her arms still wrapped around my neck, we both fell to the floor, which made sounds loud enough to attract the attention of the others.

"Way to knock a girl off her feet," she smiled and started to get up. I mumble something incoherent that even I didn't understand. The mistletoe dropped from where it was hanging onto her. She picked it up and started to laugh. "It's mistlethong. They wedged the mistletoe into a thong." I looked at it and laughed as well. That was way less embarrassing than thinking of my falling on her.

She smiled at me. "I need to say goodbye to some other people. Merry Christmas," she smiled, threw the mistlethong at me and walked away. She had only taken two steps before she half-turned. "You know, if you want to get into my Christmas stockings, you're going to have to do better than a mistlethong kiss every three years. A girl can only wait so long dating her second choices." And with that she walked away.

I stood upright, stuffed the mistlethong into my pocket and walked over to the free beer table. Holiday traditions are magic. Even if you're a Jew and the traditions aren't yours.

Author's notes: *Another early story with the challenge I gave myself to work a thong into the story. Not having it being worn gave me some freedom to change its function. And truthfully,* *most stories involving a thong are really about a relationship between two people...or should be.*

FOOD FOR THOUGHT

Over ten thousand items line the supermarket shelves and the only thing I can think of is imagining how good of a kisser she is.

I have been following her in the supermarket for five minutes now, trying to be subtle. To disguise my actions, I make a show of feeling the tomatoes and squeezing the peaches. I announce out loud that the peaches are hard today but none of the people nearby, including her, look my way. I don't really care...I hate tomatoes and peaches. I have been arranging my entire food shopping trip around her and her movements.

There's no logical explanation why I am following her. She IS pretty, there's no question. Her long blonde hair moves in a rich wave when she moves. But there's something else I can't explain. The way she moves her shoulders as she reaches for items. I am unable to stop watching her ass as she walks away from me and out of sight to another aisle. Suddenly I have butterflies. You would think that a guy my age would have outgrown them, or could at least control them. You would think wrong.

She leaves the produce to go down the cereal aisle. I wait a few seconds before pushing my cart to the one she is in and pretend to examine the ingredients of the healthier cereal boxes. No sense alienating her this early by having her see my usual fare of raspberry pop-tarts and fruit snacks that are clearly not just given their name.

I don't stare at her directly. I fear it like staring into an eclipse and going blind, so I look out the corner of my eye and from the reflection off of glass bottles I lift from the shelves and carefully test viewing angles. She seems too preoccupied to notice me and why should she: she's beautiful and I'm just...me. Jeans, a Beatles t-shirt and a salt and pepper beard I should have trimmed three days ago. I want to abandon my cart, run out to the car to at least brush my hair. But by the time I come back, she may have left the market. So the best I can do is stalk her, trying to make it look like a coincidence.

She exits to shop in another aisle. I wait the perfunctory five seconds and enter the aisle from the opposite end. *Eyes, stare at her eyes* I repeat in my head and then accidentally bang my cart into hers. She looks up and smiles.

"Oops, looks like a head on," she says

"Looks like mine isn't on." I reply and see from her expression I am not near as clever as I thought I was being. "I mean, I should watch where I am going."

"No harm done. Carts are made strong and I didn’t have eggs in the cart." She smiled and began to walk away.

I'm desperate to continue the conversation we started. "Do you know much about this?" I call after her, and without looking, grab an arbitrary product off the. She stares at me and the laughs.

"Yes. Probably a little more than you. What do you plan on using it for?"

"Oh you know...the usual," and I move my eyes to my hand to see I have grabbed a box of heavy flow maxi pads. I look back at her then back at the pads. "Oh, I grabbed the wrong thing."

"I sure hope so," and she turned and pushed her cart the other direction.

By the time she hit frozen foods, I know that I am running out of time. Not only is the next stop the checkout but the coincidence now is creepy, even to me. I screw up enough bravery that I think I can make initial contact. I try hard to avoid staring at her areas affected most by the frozen food temperatures.

I smile as my cart approaches hers.

"Not going to hit me again, are you?" she asks with a smile that could melt all of the frozen foods in the store..

"No…not unless you hit on me…..on my cart, I mean, hit my cart." I really need to go learn to speak.

"A lady wouldn't do that."

"No, of course not. I just mean…" and again I am at a loss for words. I smile. She smiles. And we proceed in different directions. I realize there are still a few things I need to get, things I have forgotten as I was following her. I race up and down the aisles but by the time I finish, she is nowhere in the market. I curse, promising that if I ever see her again, I will be braver.

By the time I got out of the market, she was there beside the car with her cart, groceries still in the cart. My car was parked two aisles away, but I chose a route to it that placed me next to her.

"Are you okay, do you need any help?"

"Well now that you ask, a little help would be great. I pulled a muscle in yoga and am having trouble lifting things."

"Then let me help you," I responded as she opened the hatch to her car. I silently loaded the groceries, desperately trying out conversations in my head. Only after the last bag was in and the hatch was closed did I turn and say, "It's a good thing I came along."

"Oh, I had two other offers for help. I just thought I could do better. I was right."

There was silence as I tried to understand the implications of her reply.

"So I should thank you in some way for helping me. I have enough groceries to make a really nice dinner and you look like a really nice guy. Maybe if you brought a really nice bottle of wine, we could have a really nice evening." Silence as I stare at her. "Just nod if you like the idea," she added.

I nodded slowly and then kept nodding like a bobblehead.

"Attraction is a funny thing. You can't explain it. I don't do this with just anyone. You are the first. I saw you the minute you walked in the market. I knew I wouldn't be happy if I let you leave without talking to you." Then she reached and took my hand, pushed herself into me slightly and kissed me on the lips. She pulled back. "My phone number is on the paper in your hand. Call me in an hour. Dinner is at 6." And she got in her car and drove away.

It turns out, the answer to the thought is that she kisses damn good.

Author's notes: *More than my other piece revolving around guys and their attraction to women, this one was well received by readers who identified with the feeling. Or maybe they just got accustomed to reading my pieces where the guy is unsure of himself in his pursuit of a woman.*

The first draft seemed stalkerish to my first group of critique readers, which ruined the true nature of the story. The change of just a few lines made it much better received the second time around. Thank goodness for honest feedback during critique!

THE CASE OF THE WIDOW BIALOFSKI

The framed theater posters on the wall, twenty of them, were a resume of the man's career. A single book of matches on the desk from The Black Cat caught my eye. Suddenly, the truth slams me like a lead pipe to the back of the head. Actually, it may have been a lamp. It didn't matter, the result was the same and it all faded to black.

When I came to, I was strapped to a metal chair with tie-offs that would make a sailor proud. Car headlights shined in my eyes, making me squint. I had played this entire scene wrong. It was anyone's guess whether Lois Hazard's favorite son would ever celebrate the 1948 New Year.

I recognized the over-applied perfume belonging to one Betty Bialofski, wife of the recently dead Gerald Bialofski and, not coincidentally, my latest client. The muzzle that pressed against the base of my skull spoke volumes before I heard her husky voice.

"You've gotten a bit too close to the truth," she said.

"It's what happens when you hire a good shamus," I

replied. There had been something suspicious about our first meeting, but the money had made me look past that little warning voice in my head. A beautiful woman in black, mourning her husband, wanting me to look into his death. There was a chance, I thought, for good pay and maybe a bonus.

"I had heard you were washed up. That you were good ***before*** ..."

Before was the placeholder for "before the shooting" and "before the drinking." It's hard to live up to a reputation...or live one down.

I realized, too late, that my hiring was a cover-up. And what better coverup that than a private dick hired by the widow?"

"How did you figure it out?" She coughed from the cigarette she obviously just lit.

"Little things like that, the cough. That's the cough from a new smoker, not one with a twenty-year habit."

"Damn nasty things. I told HER to stop, that the things would kill her."

"Me thinks thou dost protest too much." She walked around to face me, dressed in mourning black, veil to toe, the same as each time I met her. "And the perfume," I continued. "The first time, it was just a hint. The second time, overpowering, like someone who hadn't had years to figure out how much to use. Or was using it to distract. Then, the framed posters and the match book. Not the type of bar a lady like Betty Swanson would visit. Or ANY REAL lady for that matter."

She lifted her veil. The headlights silhouetted the figure. I couldn't see the face but it didn't matter. I knew it was Gerald standing there. "You have no idea how carefully this was planned."

"Was she part of it, or just another victim?"

"She was part of it…in the beginning. I needed her to play her role." He laughed at his own joke. "But certainly not long term. I told her we would split the money and she could start a new life with someone more suited to her…leanings and so could I. She agreed."

"But in the end?" I questioned.

"In the end, why should I split the money with her? I could easily play **both** parts. The dead husband and the grieving widow." I strained against the ropes. "Marines," he said. "The knots will hold far longer than you have to live." He leveled the Colt at me.

"And now?" I asked.

"Poor "Betty Bialofski" takes her insurance check and goes off to England to start a new life, never to be heard from again. And Gerald begins a new life under a new identity in a more…liberal environment."

"And the real Betty?"

"In Key West, waiting for a paycheck that will never show. But that's what you get for trying to fake a death and cheat insurance companies, isn't it? Disappointment."

"Disappointment," I nodded. "Plans go sideways. Like her being **here**?" and I stared over his shoulder.

"Stupid trick, that won't wo…." But his voice was drowned out by the echo of three rounds. He fell to the ground with his blood creating a dark pool around him.

"Nice shooting," I told the real Betty.

"I had a lot of free time while he was out catting around. I filled it with target practice." I smiled. I liked this woman. "He sent me away to wait for him, but if he didn't show up to split the cash, what would I do? Turn myself in saying that I faked his death?" She smiled as she untied me. "So what do WE do with the body?"

I rubbed my wrists where the tight ropes had chaffed them. "It seems to me that the insurance company believes he fell overboard. I say that it was just delayed and I can still feel good about confirming it. As long as I get...what? 15%. After all, you did hire me."

"And saved your life."

"Which wouldn't have been in danger if not for you."

"Tomato, To-mah-to." We dumped the body in the back of his own car and drove to the boat slip.

She turned to me. "You know, I still have the place in Key West. Maybe you'd like to join me for a month or three. Who knows, maybe they have need for a detective agency. I have some money I need to invest. And a girl likes a smart companion."

Now that's the kind of bonus I'm talking about.

Author's notes: *Fitting a noir story into flash fiction format was a huge challenge. You just don't have the time (words) to develop the mystery/suspense behind the situation. My solution was to almost immediately drop the shamus into his situation and have him quickly reveal the complete backstory in thoughts and conversation. Hopefully I accomplished that.*

One interesting fact is that the club mentioned in the beginning of the story was an early gay club in the city. Not that most people would recognize the name, but it was a fun fact to drop into the story.

Two details did change, again as the result of feedback from my writers group. The Widow Swanson became the Widow Bialofski. I don't remember why, but I changed it without question. And the detective name switched from Danger to Hazard due to Danger already having being used by Firesign Theatre for their detective story.

AND THE CROWD ROARED

"Why is there a soccer ball in the shower?" I ask my then-six-year-old son Seth. The soccer ball is a new addition to the usual assortment of action figures and nerf guns. The shower is oversized and can accommodate two people and a few child toys…and apparently, a soccer ball.

"I invented a new game. Come play with me." Any game that encourages a six year old to take a shower on a regular basis without begging, pleading or threatening is a good one. So I tell him "okay." He turns on the water and strips down before entering the shower.

Then I see him kick and hear the sound of the ball bouncing off the shower walls. "See?" and he explains the rules to me. "I kick the ball and it bounces off the wall. If I block it from hitting the wall behind me, I win. If I miss, the ball wins."

Two things become immediately obvious. The first is that the kid is an inventive genius. The second is a less happy revelation. My son is an only child and lacks playmates. He is adopted and one of the roughest stories of adoption most people have ever heard. The time and money it took to make it happen made a second adoption impossible to consider. He's surrounded by a loving family but it is moments like these that I feel guilty for not being able to give him a brother or sister.

So, after watching him for a minute, I strip down too and enter the shower. "How about if you play against me?" I offer and see a smile light up his face. We lightly kick the ball at each other in the confined space, trying to get it past the legs blocking the wall. The cascading water almost sounds like the sound of a crowded auditorium…if you pretend a bit.

The tight space and the state of undress inspired an important rule on my part. "No aiming above the knees. Please." He nodded and added his own. "And no tickling me so you can get the ball past me." And the game began in earnest.

Our score was five-four and the crowd is cheering when the shower door suddenly swings open. "What are you two doing?" We hadn't heard his mom enter the bathroom or call for us.

My "Ummm," is interrupted by my son's direct explanation. "We're playing Shower Soccer." She stares at the two of us for a few seconds before shaking her head, shutting the shower door and walking away.

I guess some things only a father and son can understand.

Author's notes: *A perfect story to end this volume. Another true story with just a few embellishments. I think this one offers fatherhood and love wrapped up in a neat little package.*

As with all stories, it uses only the number of words it needs to be told and nothing more. I like that it packs so much in so few words.

https://www.youtube.com/watch?v=riJOUYNqduE&t

ABOUT THE AUTHOR

Gary Zenker is a marketing strategist and tactical implementer. He's written dozens of business and marketing plans, hundreds and hundreds of ads and endless copy for brochures, web sites, white papers, speeches, and …well, you get the idea. His work has received awards in multiple industries. It's also produced sales and profits for the companies who employed him.

In addition, his fiction writing has won a couple of awards and was selected in an Oxford University Press contest as their winning entry on one of his favorite topics: the super powers of ordinary people.

Gary founded and runs the Main Line Writers Group in King of Prussia, PA and the Wilmington Writers Group in Glen Mills, PA, helping writers to better their craft and reach their writing goals.

Gary is also the developer of WritersBloxx, a storytelling party game and writers prompt tool. Get more information at www.WritersBloxx.com.

www.GaryZenkerStoryteller.com

garyzenker@gmail.com

Main Line Writers Group:

www.MainLineWritersGroup.com

https://www.meetup.com/Main-Line-Writers

Wilmington Writers Group

www.WilmingtonWritersGroup.com

https://www.meetup.com/Wilmington-Writers-Group

PODCAST: 999 WORDS OR LESS

www.999WordsOrLess.com

A weekly podcast focused on flash fiction with guest authors reading and discussing their work. Hosted by Gary Zenker. Scheduled for 2018 launch.

Printed in Dunstable, United Kingdom

80375121R00107